COREAGEOUS

EMPOWERING STORIES AND SKILL SETS
FOR A HEART-CENTERED LIFE

COREAGEOUS

EMPOWERING STORIES AND SKILL SETS
FOR A HEART-CENTERED LIFE

VALERIE J. WALSH

COREPRESS

Coreageous: Empowering Stories and Skill Sets for a Heart-Centered Life
First edition 2024

Copyright © COREPRESS

For permission requests: vwalsh1414@gmail.com

ISBN: 979-8-218-38565-1 (paperback)
ISBN: 979-8-218-38566-8 (ebook)

Book design by G Sharp Design, LLC

For Bailey and Collin

May you always feel empowered to live life from your CORE. Trust in the strength of your own heart-center, a place where you can find God. He made you, loves you, and wants you to believe in yourself and your ability to live a COREAGEOUS life of purpose.

May you also always know the profound love and support I will always have for you.

CORE CONTENTS

My Story 1

Chapter 1   **CORE-restoration**. 13
             My Return to Health

Chapter 2   **Tune in Tokyo** 31
             Tuning Inward, To Tune Out The Stressors In My Life

Chapter 3   **Spiritual Quest** 55
             My Unindoctrinated Union with God

Chapter 4   **86'd Words**. 91
             The Three Words I Loathe

Chapter 5   **CORE-peeps**. 105
             Beautiful Friendships Are Like Beautiful Music

Chapter 6   **Extroverted Introvert** .123
             Host Then Ghost...Please Come Over,
             but Leave by Six O'clock

Chapter 7   **COREAGEOUS Culture**. 133
             COREAGEOUS Vibe and Together We'll Thrive

Chapter 8   **Remaining Curious** 159
             The Importance of Remaining Curious,
             Coachable, and Passionate

Chapter 9   **Pivot** 173
When We Cling to What We Know,
We Miss the Chance to Grow

Chapter 10   **Zenemies** 197
The Peeps Who Zap Your Zen Are Not Your Friends

Chapter 11   **I Like Being an Outsider** 213
Grace Among This Place

Chapter 12   **Irish Twins** 229
The Luck of the Irish

Chapter 13   **What it Means to be COREAGEOUS** 249
The Heart, the OG of Bravery

Chapter 14   **CORE-strong Tool Kit** 271
Progress, Setback, Repeat.
Practice, Practice, Practice

MY STORY

WHAT HAPPENS TO a person after they are shattered? In my story, there was a time in my life when I endured an ocean full of relentless waves that I was wholly unprepared for. Often, I referred to this period in my life as "my shitstorm." A culmination of events that knocked me to my knees, breaking my heart into a million pieces. I experienced years of aftershocks that damaged my physical, emotional, and spiritual self. Ultimately, I made a choice to do the necessary work to turn my pain into purpose, while at the same time, no longer allowing it to take center stage in my life.

After losing my mother to suicide—a time in my life that I wrote about in great detail in my memoir, *Shattered to the Core*—I became determined to rebuild my **CORE**, stronger than ever before. I am not talking about a six-pack here. The **CORE** that I am referring to is my heart and the person I am now in the aftermath of great trauma.

I surrendered to the realization that the way I lost my mom will never be okay. After she died by suicide in 2013, I began to binge drink once again to numb myself—only this time trauma on top of trauma was added to the mix. In the span of four very tough years, I endured a double mastectomy with reconstruction and my fifteen-year-old daughter was diagnosed with stage three thyroid cancer.

Today, although I'm only 5' 2", I stand tall in my truth. The good, the bad, the sad, the ugly, and the amusing. Today, I am a woman who is better prepared—physically, emotionally, and spiritually—for the waves that are sure to continue to ebb and flow in my life. I have discovered that truly living your life and experiencing every emotion to the fullest requires work so you will have the strength to ride out those waves.

Now, I consider myself very blessed in life to have encountered such waves. I've learned valuable lessons from both the tsunamis that were strong and ferocious in their power to try and overtake me to the swells I have been lucky enough to catch a ride on. Everything has shown me that nothing is permanent. Every state of being is a momentary experience.

I wanted to learn what it would be like to be in the ocean. I wanted to learn how to tap into the calm space underneath all of the chaos of life. The turbid water at the surface was too muddy for me to live in any longer, and I couldn't breathe there. I wanted to learn how to dive deep into my heart's **CORE** and recognize the moment I became aware of a wave—off in the distance—trying to take me down. I wanted to learn what I needed to do to remove anything that restricted the light from penetrating through the surface problems. I wanted that light to shine within me once again.

This book is about that deep dive into the **CORE** of who I always was, but momentarily lost. It is about who I have become, and who I am still becoming. It is about a woman who is better equipped to handle her life because she remembers her resilience, shares her vulnerability, asks for help when she needs it, and helps others when she is able. This book is not to preach what I believe is right or wrong, but rather what I feel is true and authentic for me.

To rise, to fall. To be strong, to be vulnerable. To be beautiful, to be ugly. To be serious, to be funny. To be human. To experience it all, and to share my story is what I love to do. It is how I connect with others, and it is how I have healed from being shattered.

Through storytelling, and sharing our experiences in life, we create connections with one another. These connections are more important than ever before, especially in a world of instant gratification and convenience. Our stories turn our immensely big world into something small enough to fit into the palm of our hands, much like the angel worry stone I used to carry with me after my mother died. Publishing my first book proved to me that by sharing our stories, we work together as one human team to feel less alone in our humanity.

Sharing some of the darkest days of my life in ***Shattered to the Core*** connected me with people I never would have met otherwise, and it gave me the opportunity to hear their stories. It also reacquainted me with those I had known, but who now felt comfortable opening up to me, feeling unashamed, and unburdened by embarrassment. There is power in truth, and when you share it with another human being, that is true intimacy. You don't have to do it by authoring a book, speaking on a podcast, or sharing on any type of public platform, as I have often felt called to do. It can happen in the simplest of ways.

Sharing can be done through meeting a friend for coffee or going on a walk. It can happen any time that you listen to someone and respond kindly. This type of intimacy—of truly being open, present, and vulnerable—came to me in many places before I put pen to paper or before publicly speaking out. I found connection, support, and healing on hiking trails, in hot yoga studios, on my road bike, and through phone calls. I found it in church, out of church, in the gym, and at work. I also found it in any venue willing to rent space to my recovery program, where other like-minded people had the willingness to share their personal stories. You see, my true authenticity was revealed to me when I got sober from alcohol. My light began to shine again through my sobriety.

Before there was any book for me to write, there was a Big Book for me to read where others were brave enough to share their stories, and it inspired me to dive down into the **CORE** of who I am, and who I am meant to be. The woman I lost for a little while was still there. That reminder, that wake-up call, came after watching my mother die a hard and lonely death. It was then that I began to explore what I needed to do to feel true peace amidst the seemingly unbearable waves of life. How I needed to strengthen my **CORE**, stronger than any six-pack stomach I used to focus on.

Long before this word was used in the title of two of my books, it was an acronym I referenced while I worked as a personal trainer and coach. I used the word **CORE** for goal setting. The acronym stood for:

> **C**   Challenge (personal goal)
>
> **O**   Obstacles (things standing in the way of your goal)
>
> **R**   Reason (your why/your purpose)
>
> **E**   Exercises (training plan)

Now, almost twenty years after **CORE** was birthed into existence and used for training my clients, this gem of a word has morphed into so much more. **CORE** is the center of who we are: our heart center. For me, it is the place that I can tap into, where I feel most connected to God.

CORE, the original meaning of the word, was derived in the late fourth century as a noun. It came about from the Old French Coeur, meaning "core of fruit" and more literally, the heart.

All of the years I was a **CORE** coach, training countless people to achieve the six-pack of their desire, would lead me to the deeper meaning of what the word means for me, and many others, today.

Now, this acronym stands for:

C   Challenge (personal goal or crisis)

O   Outcome (what is the outcome you want)

R   Reason (your why/your purpose)

E   Execution (what tools will you pick-up for the outcome you want)

My former and present clients believe that their **CORE** is also the heart of who they are. A place they are capable of tapping into in order to be their strongest self—in mind, body, and spirit— otherwise known as **CORE-strong** in our fitness community.

Although a part of my soul died the day my mother did, so did the many layers of false truths that I needed to shed to take back my life. As the murkiness began to fade, my light began to shine, leading me toward a better path through life. A path that still continues to have bumps, twists, and turns, but one that I will never have to walk alone.

No, *it* would never be okay, but in time, *I* would be okay. I would learn that time only heals if I have the diligence to do the work that is necessary to allow for healing, and I did not have to do it alone.

Eventually, I would become the woman my mother could have been had she lived long enough—the miracle of the possibility of a full and peaceful existence.

The feather on the cover of this book represents my beautiful mother through the Native American belief that:

"FEATHERS APPEAR WHEN ANGELS ARE NEAR."

Today, I carry the most beautiful parts of my mother in me and honor her by turning my pain into purpose. My mother was kind, generous, loving, funny, and creative. She was hard-working, resourceful, smart, and so much more. I also carry an inner peace despite never fully knowing if she is, in fact, okay, having let go of any resentments from losing my mother in a manner that was sudden and traumatic.

So, how does one rebuild a life after losing one's mother to suicide and both breasts to a mastectomy? Through trial and error. Through honesty and accountability. Through faith and hope. Through reading and writing. Through speaking and listening. Through crying and laughing. Through pain and joy. Through solitude and connection. I share all of these in this empowering book.

Life is not meant to be perfect. We are not meant to never experience pain. God forbid we do experience pain— we try to numb it with any method we can find: alcohol, drugs, eating disorders, overspending, gambling, distractions, you name it. We all have our default vices that we reach for.

Perspective has been a wonderful gift, and in this book, I share some of the views I gained about events that have happened in both my past and present. The **CORE** of how I have kept myself from falling down the same rabbit hole my mother did. How the little things—like trying my best to do the next right thing—have led to the bigger things—like being an author and public speaker. Taking the next right step has led to more opportunities than I ever could have possibly dreamed for myself.

What is the **CORE** of who we are? Such an important question to ask ourselves. What makes us light up inside and fires us up? What excites us or drains us? What nourishes our heart or depletes it? What makes us **CORE-strong** in order to be **COREAGEOUS?**

Our **CORE,** anatomically speaking, is the part of the human body that is responsible for protecting our spine. Metaphorically speaking, without a strong **CORE,** we become spineless and weak of character, and eventually, our light will begin to dim.

The same can be said when we stick to its original meaning referring to the center of fruit. Like the **CORE** of an apple, we die a little more each time, if we allow things or people who are not meant for us to keep taking bites off us, and this woman wants to live! This woman no longer allows her pain to be the center stage of her life, but rather the platform she propels herself forward from.

This book is filled with funny, embarrassing, and relatable life lessons of some of the **COREAGEOUS** and not-so-outrageous ways I have chosen to live a life no longer in fear of disappointing others or myself. In the final chapter of this book, I will share a summary of each particular tool I personally use, in the chapter titled: **CORE-strong Tool Kit.** Sharing is caring, and this book is possible because of the many people in my life who shared their time, experiences, and expertise with me. The tools that work for me may or may not work for you. Pick-up the ones that do, carry them with you, and pass them along to another because THAT is what life is about—making meaningful connections and sharing our hearts.

This book is for you, my **CORE-peeps**, because if you're reading it, you are likely one of them.

To help you get the most out of this book, please review the following CORE items:

CORE-NERSTONES. Not quite a stone, but rather a little nugget of truth, placed in the margins, throughout each story. These little gems of truth are takeaways for you to keep for yourself, as well as share with others. Hashtag away and spread these nuggets around for other peeps to enjoy! #COREnerstones

CORE-RELATIONS. You will find these at the end of each chapter. They are questions for you to ask yourself. Key points from the story to which you may relate. Included are blank pages for you to write your answers or to jot down any thoughts you may have for yourself. This is a good opportunity to also share within a group setting.

COREAGEOUS CHALLENGE. After you've read each chapter and taken a moment to reflect on how you may relate to the story I have shared, I challenge you to take steps toward personal growth and living a heart-centered life for yourself.

CORE Glossary of Terms:

CORE: My heart-center. The place where I can turn inward and feel most connected to God, in order to be my authentic self.

COREAGEOUS: To be your authentic self. To be true to your heart. To speak honestly and openly about who you are and what you are feeling, so that you may be strong enough to help yourself or others in need.

CORE-nerstones: Little nuggets of truth, within each story.

CORE-relations: How you may identify with the story.

COREAGEOUS Challenge: Small steps toward living a heart-centered life.

CORE-peeps: People, community, family, folks, humans, kin... you get the picture.

CORE-restoration: Otherwise known as self-care.

CORE-strong: When you feel your strongest of mind, body, and spirit, creating a peaceful heart-center.

CORE-values: The things that we choose to prioritize as important.

CORE-strong Tool Kit: The specific tools used to hold on to the strong foundation of who we are and what we want out of life. Skill Sets that are practiced to be **CORE-strong** in order to be **COREAGEOUS.**

CHAPTER ONE

CORE-RESTORATION

My Return to Health

MY SOBRIETY HAS to come first. It is that simple. When I overcomplicate or overthink things, I risk the peace that I have worked so hard to gain. When I put my sobriety first, all of the other things in my life seem to fall into place: mentally, emotionally, physically, and spiritually. My sobriety was my first real solid step toward my **CORE-restoration**, my return to health. This is why I feel a strong need to begin here, with just how and why I made this decision.

As a writer, I want to share as many pertinent details as possible to convey my point. As a person in a recovery program, however, I do my best to respect the element of anonymity when sharing my story. Here, I will strive to find balance between the two as I share my stories and experiences throughout this book.

The last time I had a drink was September 16, 2017. Some of the literature that I have read describes alcoholism as a "cunning, baffling, and powerful disease," and I agree with this statement. For thousands of years, humans have struggled with addiction, and many viewed this struggle as a lack of willpower. Anyone who knew me as a toddler or a teen would agree that I have no shortage of willpower over most things—unfortunately, alcohol was not one of them. When it came to binge drinking, I was powerless.

Alcoholism looks different for everyone, and I would not dare try to describe the disease as a whole, but rather what it looked like for me, when I was drinking.

I was a binge drinker—a "work hard, play harder" type of gal. Go to work, clean the house, make the breakfasts, pack the lunches, make the dinners, organize the schedules, keep the order, juggle the balls, care for the family, care for the friends—a "do all the things" type of gal. Then, and only then—when everything was in its place, and everyone had a smile on their face—I felt I had earned my right to let loose on the weekends—that I had earned it. Not every weekend, but when I did, I would never stop at just one drink. I drank to get drunk. To be the life of the dinner party, the one to answer all of the trivia questions, slurring my words through the answers, but feeling so smart. Smarter with alcohol.

Prettier with alcohol. Calmer with alcohol. Funnier with alcohol. Indestructible with alcohol. I was more than, until it made me feel less than.

I learned it was the rituals surrounding the act of planning my drinking that were my red flags. It was the obsession of when and where it was safe to let loose, and the lies I would tell myself (such as, *It's okay to drink tonight, both kids are at sleepovers*) that were all signs I had an issue with alcohol. It was the mental gymnastics that played over and over in my head, justifying why it was okay that I drank, convincing myself that I didn't drink like my mother (never alone or as often) that talked me out of believing I was an alcoholic.

This is how the disease tricked me. It convinced me that because I could still manage my life and keep everything in balance (or so I thought) there was no way I had an issue. But I did. Truthfully, I drank alcoholically from the start. Likely for me, it started with early exposure to drugs and alcohol within my family from a very early age. Coming home to a house wreaking of marijuana and to a mother who was doing her best to sober up from getting high or at times day drinking. Perhaps my alcohol abuse was due to unaddressed childhood trauma, lack of purpose or self-esteem, or all of these things combined.

Whatever the root cause was, by the time I made the decision to stop drinking, my disease was starting to affect my emotional and mental health. I would wake up in a cold sweat after a night of drinking. It was no longer just a hangover I was experiencing—these were panic attacks. The attacks were heightened by the drinking and would lead to several days of more panic, anxiety, and waves of depression. It was as if the alcohol that I put into my body was the gasoline that these mental disorders were fueled by.

I cannot safely drink alcohol, and I have had to accept what alcohol can do to my mind, body, and **CORE**. I am well aware of its poison and potential to kill me if I let it in again.

I make the choice each day to return to health. I refuse to let the toxic things, like alcohol, into my life. I will not give them the chance to stunt my growth or dim my light. My sobriety has presented opportunities, earned through hard work and faith, both professionally and personally. I believe that faith is an action word, and I have to act on my faith each day to better set myself up for success.

Whether or not you struggle with addiction issues, you will relate in some way because these empowering stories are useful for ALL peeps, not just those of us in recovery. The truth is, it is not just the abuse of alcohol that is poisonous to our **CORE**. It is anything or anyone that robs us of our internal peace, placing us in survival mode rather than a mode where we may thrive.

By the time I made the decision to get sober, I was far from feeling healthy in mind, body, and spirit. In fact,

I was merely surviving, not thriving. Thriving was something I wanted for myself, and deep down inside my **CORE**, I knew I deserved it.

Sobriety was the first real step I took toward my own **CORE-restoration,** otherwise known as self-care.

Type the phrase, "self-care" into Google, and you will see just how important it is—and together we will continue its momentum of being a leading term trending on the internet. For the purpose of this book, I will continue to refer to it as **CORE-restoration.** The ironic thing about **CORE-restoration** is that most of us, including myself, go outside of ourselves to look for it. That is exactly what I was doing when I was drinking. I was trying to look to outside things to feel better, or at times, to not feel at all.

The truth is, everything that we need to take care of ourself lies within our own intuition.

The truth is, everything that we need to take care of ourself lies within our own intuition. We all have the ability to tune in and listen to what our **CORE** is telling us. **CORE-restoration** is being able to take care of what we need, so that we are able to give to others. To truly be present for our family and friends or to be a good employee, manager, or owner of a business. To be a good peep in general, we must first take care of what we require—then we can be of service to others.

CORE-restoration. Let's break this word down.

CORE. I described this word in my Introduction. I refer to my heart as my **CORE.**

Restoration. What is it exactly? Spiritually speaking, many faiths will agree that the Biblical definition of the word restoration may be interpreted to mean a renewal of one's spiritual faith. That restoration is a returning of our hearts toward God, an understanding of our spiritual purpose on earth, and a return to health.

My ability to enjoy life and feel comfortable in my own skin is a direct result of my sobriety. This gift—this restoration—gave me clarity. My purpose became crystal clear to me. Sharing my hardships, but more importantly, the tools I have used to heal my mind, body, and spirit, became my purpose. Writing, coaching, speaking, and volunteering, along with mental health advocacy, are all part of the service work that helps to keep me sober and also provides me with a life where I am thriving rather than just surviving. Whenever I perform activities of service, my soul lights up. This state of mind is what psychologists refer to as "flow."

Flow, simply put, is when I feel myself becoming totally immersed in an activity. When in this state of mind, I don't feel like I am working, but rather, using my skills— my God-given gifts—to thrive in this life. To feel restored. These gifts came out of sobriety and getting honest with myself. Some of these gifts were lying within me already, such as leading, and became enhanced when I quit drinking. My sobriety and the people within the program I utilize, as well as the licensed professionals I work with and learn from, are responsible for this transformation and my restoration to health. None of it is solely my own.

While I am aware of what I need for my own **CORE-restoration** and the work I must do each day to protect it, I am also aware of and grateful for those who have helped me return to health of mind, body, and spirit. One of the most crucial truths for you to realize is that you are not alone in your struggles. Understanding this can make a significant difference in overcoming whatever you may be dealing with. Be sure to surround yourself with encouraging people who will provide you with the right kind of support to help you move forward. If you are struggling with mental health and/or addiction issues, I hope you will have the willingness to reach out to a licensed professional for help, who will be able to review different resources that are available to help aid in your recovery. I did, and still do to this day. My approach to my sobriety, and connecting back to my authentic self, right from the start, took shape as more of a wellness approach. Likely because of my years of experience in the health and fitness industry, this path appealed to me. It was no surprise that I started to thrive and heal when I was open to any program that would offer connection with other people who were going through similar experiences. That connection was KEY to my health. Connection, as well as keeping up with exercising, talking with a licensed professional as needed and welcoming other practices that would help me to feel empowered and take ownership of my return to health.

When we start to pay genuine attention to our needs and begin working on ourselves, some may judge and label it selfish or self-centered. Giving attention to what we need is not selfish or self-centered. I used to struggle with this concept. The thought of putting myself first was uncomfortable because, from a very young age, I was taught to believe that wasn't valuable.

Giving attention to what we need is not selfish or self-centered.

It was programmed into my DNA until I learned how to reprogram the decades of life lessons that would prevent me from becoming the woman in my **CORE**—the woman I was meant to be.

My mother put everyone else's needs before her own rather than address her own addiction and mental health issues; both were a product of the time she lived in and growing up watching these poor choices built them into my DNA. Each experience was a building block, and their collective power bonded together to form who I became. But the good news is, no matter your past, you still get to choose who you will become and how you will grow.

Society has programmed us to believe that putting our own needs first is selfish and self-centered. Our society is built on guilt—in the workplace, at home, in schools, in church—the guilt is everywhere. It wasn't until I learned how to tune into what I needed for my own **CORE-restoration** that I finally found the peace I was searching for in all those false truths outside of myself.

CORE-restoration is the opposite of selfishness or self-centeredness. Selfishness is the desire to take from others, where caring for yourself allows you to restore your own energy and be of service in this complicated, high burnout-rate world we live in. Self-centeredness is only focusing on your own thoughts, activities, or interests. However, when you take the time to learn what you need to be a whole and healthy person, then you are able to be authentically interested and curious about other people's thoughts, activities, and interests in life. Before giving it away so freely to others, you must first restore your energy, your own heart center, to avoid burning out and preserve the authenticity of self.

To tune in and truly listen to my **CORE**, my intuition, took discipline. My **CORE** is the place within myself where I feel connected to God. Self-discipline is a learned skill I practice daily that allows me to tune into my own needs or what God is trying to tell me.

If you are reading this and cringing at the word discipline, in the same way I cringe when someone uses particular words that I loathe (you will learn what those words are soon enough), let me shed some light on this magical word.

Discipline

Discipline has gained a reputation of harshness, of punishment, when truly all it means is to learn.

The word "discipline" is from the Latin word disciplina, meaning instruction and training. It is derived from the root word discert—"to learn." It is **NOT** a synonym for punishment, as most of us have been programmed through schooling to believe (especially if you have ever been called down to the principal's office for disciplinary action). If you have a memory of that, it is understandable why you may cringe when hearing this word. Truthfully, I used to dislike it as well, until something, or rather someone, changed my attitude.

When I learned that discipline was not something that was done to me, but rather a blessing to be able to practice for myself, well…I couldn't get enough of the damn stuff!

Along with my sobriety program, I started using wellness podcasts as a tool to help build a stronger mindset. I had plenty of time for this on my 90-minute commute to work each day!

Algorithms of what I had been listening to in this last decade, were now starting to formulate and one morning on my "You Might Like" Apple Podcast Suggestions, a show called *DETAIL THERAPY* with Amy Landino popped up while I was setting up my device for my long drive.

On this particular episode, Amy had Tim Kight as a special guest on her show.

Tim Kight is the founder and CEO of Focus 3, a firm whose mission is to help people maximize their performance through discipline-driven leadership, culture, and behavior.

At least, that is what his "About Us" page says on his website, but truth be told, had Amy led with that statement, I may have tuned out, as the thought of listening to something that may have been related only to corporate work culture, or so I assumed at first, would not have been interesting to me at the time.

However, Amy hooked me right away when she shared with her listeners that Tim is passionate about teaching others how to respond to life's events and developing the skill set needed for the life that you want. I was so curious to hear his formula.

As a coach and personal trainer, I realize that most successful athletes, teams, and clients follow some sort of formula or plan. Besides, I am on a mission to learn and remain coachable. With this mission in mind, I turned up the volume on my radio.

"What is your plan to develop the skills that you need for the life that you want?" Tim Kight shares that this is one of his favorite questions to ask his clients. *Damn!* I think to myself, as his words strike like an arrow straight into my **CORE** and prompt me to ask myself that same question.

What is my plan to develop the skills that
I need for the life that I want?

Tim's question reminds me of something I used to say to my own fitness clients, "When we cling to what we know, we miss the chance to grow."

When we cling to what we know, we miss the chance to grow.

In other words, if we hold on to the excuse that we are the way we are because of something from our past, we will miss out on the person we are capable of becoming or a life we are worthy of living.

Sometimes to change our DNA, we need a full-on blood transfusion, a new way of operating, and a new way of thinking, so to speak. Tim Kight was one of the catalysts of my stronger mindset; he inspired me to start building new blocks to bond together and form new DNA within myself.

The life that I wanted for myself included doing things I am passionate about. I wanted to live a life that had purpose, meaning, and was heart-centered—to live differently and share the possibilities of that growth with others. Frankly, I believed I was blessed with chances my mother was not given, and it would have been a disservice to her if I continued making choices that broke my heart instead of fulfilling it. By living a life that included the things I wanted, I would lead by example and set a stronger foundation for my own children, forming healthier DNA and heart centers within them, their children, and so on.

To answer Tim Kight's question, my plan was to stay sober, first and foremost, because things had only gotten better since I'd made that choice. I also realized I needed to continue learning new ways to force myself out of my comfort zone for my own personal growth and health. My plan would take diligence and discipline, both of which I thrive on now.

In my experience in the fitness industry, motivation was handed out as easily as a sweat towel during a grueling workout. If we wait to be motivated, we may never actually get to doing the things we want to accomplish, such as what is necessary for our own **CORE-restoration**. In order to hold on to the strong foundation of who we are, what we want out of life, and what is required to be good humans, we need the right tools. We must pick up these essential tools every day.

If we wait to be motivated, we may never actually get to doing the things we want to accomplish.

Each person's tools are unique to them, and I will share the particular tools that I use by sprinkling them throughout this book through storytelling.

Restoring myself to the woman I was before losing my mom was an impossible burden to place on myself, and I had to shed that burden. Besides, I really like the person I am becoming, and I continue to ask myself Tim Kight's question, *What is my plan to develop the skills that I need for the life that I want?*

After all, when we cling to what we know, we miss the chance to grow.

Today, I continue to explore various methods to keep returning to my health of mind, body, and spirit. I also continue to listen to Tim Kight and soak up the wisdom he shares in the FOCUS 3 newsletter, as well as watch him on YouTube during his *Two Minutes with TK*. But, more importantly, I embrace what Tim graciously shares from the **CORE** of who he is as he reminds me of the deeper meaning of the word.*

I also continue to educate myself on different disciplines regarding restoration. All humans change and evolve over a well-lived lifetime, and we deserve to live our best, heart-centered life. Today, I prefer diligence and discipline over motivation.

Diligence and discipline over motivation.

To become more heart-centered, it is important for all people to discover what their individual needs are and nourish them. In doing so, we may become better spouses, better partners, better parents, better role models, better employees, better managers, better friends, and overall, just better peeps.

Soon after I became sober, I was 200 hours away from studying to become a Yoga Practitioner and learning another discipline—a tool that would be one of the purest ways I learned to balance myself and tune within. My **CORE-restoration** was just beginning.

---

* To learn more about Tim Kight and the R Factor, visit his website to subscribe to his newsletter and YouTube to subscribe to Two Minutes with TK.

CORE-RELATIONS

(Questions to ask yourself)

❧ What are the things that you do presently for your own **CORE-restoration** (return to health)?

_____

_____

_____

❧ Is there something in your own life that you are holding on to that is stunting your growth or ability to move forward?

_____

_____

_____

❧ In the space provided, name one tool that you are afraid to pick-up for the life that you want for yourself. Expand on why you are afraid to pick-up this particular tool.

_____

_____

_____

COREAGEOUS Challenge: I encourage you to carve out ten minutes each day over the next three weeks dedicated to something that restores your energy, something just for you. Make it simple and attainable. The goal of this is to become disciplined about this one item so that, soon enough, it becomes a healthy habit. Here are a few examples to get you started:

- ❧ Practice mindful breathing
- ❧ Take a short walk
- ❧ Blast and belt out your favorite music

Share your progress on social media to help you stay account-able, using the hashtags: **#COREageous**, **#COREstrong,** and **#CORErestoration.** If you are more of a private person and prefer not to share online, write down your daily completion of this **COREAGEOUS Challenge** to help keep yourself on track and accountable.

CHAPTER TWO

TUNE IN TOKYO

Tuning Inward, To Tune Out The Stressors In My Life

REMEMBER THE MOVIE, *Girls Just Want to Have Fun*? It is a classically cheesy movie from the 80s where Jonathan Silverman plays an awkward (weren't we all) high schooler trying to use a stupid prank to feel a girl up. He convinces a young lady to play this party game, "Tune in Tokyo," where she places her hands behind her head, and then Johnathan Silverman's character says, "Okay Tiffany, now you gotta put your hands behind your head, yeah, that's it, that's it! Now sway back and forth and picture this: it's World War Two and our ship is in the middle of the Pacific Ocean. It's going down and our only hope is to use our short-wave radio—**TUNE IN TOKYO, TUNE IN TOKYO**," his character repeats all while twisting the young lady's nipples and pretending they are radio knobs. She immediately smacks him over the head with her purse and walks away.

She walked away. I distinctly remember watching that movie and being so impressed by this young woman's courage to stick up for herself and walk away.

Middle-School Me was not that girl. I mean, I'd like to think if some scumbag tried the "Tune in Tokyo" game on me, I would have smacked him too, but there are many times when I recall that I was too afraid to speak up or to walk away. Therefore, I put up with people and situations where I felt uncomfortable. This is something of which I am certainly not proud. I experienced many growing pains because of my social anxiety and the baseline fear that I carried around inside of me. I know now that my feelings and the choices I made as a result of them were rooted in my fear of abandonment, and therefore, I overcompensated by people pleasing.

There was the time when one of my girlfriends shoplifted right in front of me.

We were at a popular department store at our local mall when my friend decided to go into the dressing room to try on a bunch of clothing. Her plan was solid (and made during a time before there were security tags on any retail items). Inside the dressing room, she tried on the outfit she wanted to steal and kept it on underneath the outfit she was originally wearing. Boldly, she walked right out of the dressing room with the stolen clothing underneath her clothes, like it was no big deal. I said nothing because the fourteen-year-old me would have rather gone to jail over something I didn't do, than to— God forbid—have a friend mad at me.

Too many of my younger years and my friendships were guided by the ruler of our girl group. While I am not certain how said ruler was elected, I am pretty certain one of the traits needed to reign over our willing and vulnerable group was to be mean and manipulative, and this particular girl fit the criteria.

As her constituents, we followed her lead on who we were mad at, what we were wearing, where we sat for lunch, and whose house we would play at after school. This is something that I look back on and wish I had the courage to step away from. Unfortunately, I was too afraid to make waves. Far from a bully, some would probably say I was too nice. To me, I was vanilla. Not wanting to stand out, but also wanting to fit in. To be both seen, and unseen. To be everyone's friend and try to be the peacekeeper. An impossible task for any human—especially a young human trying to feel comfortable in her own skin.

This level of comfort took me a long time to accomplish. I thought it took longer than it should have, but I know now that it was the amount of time that was needed to find that level and feel at peace. Also, "should" is on the list of words that I have 86'd (a term I picked up while working in the restaurant industry, meaning "out of" or "no longer"). In the current season of my life, I have 86'd the following words, "fine," "moist,"—and most recently, "should." Now that is not to say you won't spot one of these words in this book, in fact, I have dedicated an entire chapter to those three little bitches and will waste no more time on that other little bitch from my childhood.

It took me over forty years to learn how to walk away from people, places, and things that stunted my growth. Forty years before I was **COREAGEOUS** enough to not just listen to my intuition but be able to follow through by taking action—stepping toward whatever path I needed, whatever path resonated with my true self. The character in that 80s cult classic did it without hesitation. She knew exactly who she was and what she would and would not tolerate. Choosing to listen to your inner compass requires a willingness to be who you are unapologetically, without being swayed by external opinions or judgment. It is an incredibly **COREAGEOUS** choice to make.

> *Choosing to listen to your inner compass requires a willingness to be who you are unapologetically, without being swayed by external opinions or judgment.*

When I think back to who I was at fourteen or fifteen years old (around the same age as the female character in that movie), I get very sad. Not sad with regret, rather, sad that I cannot go back in time and grab that young lady by the shoulders and say, "Stop caring so damn much about disappointing anyone and being scared that someone may get mad at you if you don't do what they want! Stand up for yourself, damn it!"

God, I was so scared, all of the time. Scared to say the wrong thing. Scared to make choices. Scared to look down at my pudgy thighs with permanent red goose pimples on them. Self-conscious, to the point that I even imagined my thighs to be much bigger than they actually were. When I would sit, I would place my hands under my legs and squeeze them tight, in the hope of making them appear smaller. Even when I was sitting, I couldn't relax in my own skin! I hated to look into the mirror at what I thought was the most hideous image of an awkwardly pale girl with bushy eyebrows and dark circles under her eyes. Cautious to truly let anyone in because I was always afraid to be myself. Terrified they would judge me and leave me. My weakened **CORE**, and my vulnerable self, could not bear it.

What I was experiencing during my early teens was more than the typical awkward years of middle school. What I was experiencing was severe social anxiety, but this was not something that was discussed in the 80s, and it also did not end in middle school. I carried this anxiety with me for decades.

When I finally made the choice to stop sleepwalking my way through life and learn what it would take to feel at ease, I was entering my forties and decided that this new decade of my life was going to look different and feel different, because well, **I was different**. I was now the daughter of a mother who died from the final symptom of her depression. Her final consequence of a life where she pretended that everything was just fine. Ugh, that word, **FINE!** Perhaps now you understand why I loathe that hideously fake word and have 86'd it from being uttered from my lips.

For fifty-nine years my mother put on her fake "fine" mask to please everyone, while any care for herself took a back seat. By the time I hit forty, I was on a mission. No longer would I pretend to feel or be something I was not. No longer would I reach for alcohol as a means to an end: end of a busy work week, end of meeting a goal, or end of any unwanted feelings creeping up inside of me. No longer would I go back in time, to fifteen-year-old me who picked up her first drink and immediately gained the false comfort of a temporary euphoria.

Act on faith, not fear.

The decision to do something different began with my sobriety, as discussed in the previous chapter, and that decision also led to other paths of resistance. Yes, you read that right—resistance. In other words, I had to step out of my comfort zone of the default characteristics that I was used to. I had to act on faith, not fear.

By this time in my life, my early forties, I had spent most of my professional career in the health and fitness industry. I worked at the front desk of gyms, taught group fitness classes, trained clients, coached running, and led outdoor boot camp programs, as well as spearheaded many innovative new fitness programs. You name it, if it was exercise-related, I learned it. I always wanted to be at the forefront of new fitness trends. If it had a certification attached to it to validate me and build my resume, that would be even better! Over the course of my health and fitness career, I had dozens of clients, hundreds of students, and countless certifications, except for one that was now constantly popping up in my head—yoga.

There was a 200-hour yoga teacher training about to begin at a local state college that would be taught by someone in my fitness circle. The teacher was a woman I had come to respect and trust over the years. Her name was Lara. The class met every Friday from 8:30 a.m., until 4:30 p.m., until we met our 200-hour requirement.

Our first Friday on the mat together as a class was very exciting and terrifying, as most new things are. Truth be told, I usually felt pretty confident going into most fitness certification classes as the focus was on resistance in the sense of muscular resistance, not anything like the resistance that we were about to dive into. This type of resistance, I would discover, would be much deeper, and in a different way, more exhausting. This would be my first of many steps down a path that would lead to something so beautiful and spiritually healing.

"Class let's put our mats in a circle and each take a turn to introduce ourselves," Lara directed. Each classmate took a few moments to state their name, where they were from, if they were married, had children, any hobbies, or fun facts—all of the usual ice breaker information people tend to talk about when getting to know one another in a group setting.

When it was my turn to speak, Lara looked over at me. "Hi Valerie!" she said with a great big smile, recognizing my familiar face among her new students. "Everyone, I know Valerie from way back in the scrunchie and leg-warmer days of working out. We both taught together at the same gym for many, many years!"

Now, I am assuming that Lara was thinking I was well prepared for this course with my decades of experience and extensive list of certifications, but inside I knew the truth—I was not prepared whatsoever. In fact, I could feel it in my **CORE.** I was nervous and totally out of my league on this one. I signed up for this yoga teacher training shortly after my mother had died. I signed up for a lot of things back then; it was just a weird time, to be honest, and like I said before, I was on a mission to try new things.

"Hi everyone, I'm Valerie. Yes, I've taught a lot of different classes, but never yoga. Actually, I haven't even taken many yoga classes, maybe two or three?"

As most typical runners (which, at that time, was my go-to activity) will tell you, we are the absolute WORST when it comes to stretching. But even from the start, during our introductions, I could sense this program was going to be about much more than just stretching.

"Anyhow, I am married, with two children, Bailey, and Collin. I signed up to take this teacher training to expand my knowledge as a fitness instructor and to work on my own physical injuries. I have a bum knee." While partly true, I mean, I really did have a bum knee and hip, what I really wanted to say to everyone was:

"Hi. My name is Valerie. I am an anxious bundle of nerves. I am already starting to sweat, and we haven't even begun any postures yet, and I hope you are able to understand me through my shaking voice. I have absolutely no freaking clue what I am doing here. My mom died not too long ago, and shortly after I went through a double mastectomy, so I am learning how to work with this new body I have after my breasts were cut off and my chest wall was expanded with metal to make a new home for two fake implants. Oh, and by the way, any previous strength I had in my upper body, well it is gone now, so don't expect me to do any downward facing dog thingies or whatever you call them in Sanskrit."

That is what I wanted to say, but instead, I put on a fake brave face and settled in.

Learning to be the confident woman (in mind, body, and **CORE**) I always knew I could be was not a linear path. Often, I fell right back into my default DNA, which is where I landed my first day on the mat with my new classmates. For their sake—and mine—

I was *fine*.

Everything continued just fine week after week during our program together, until one day when Lara invited another yoga teacher to come in and teach a type of practice that she wanted us to learn more about. The practice was called Kundalini.

The Kundalini Research Institute states that "Kundalini yoga is a dynamic blend of postures, conscious breathing, mantra, music, and meditation, which can bring you relaxation, self-healing, and elevation. It will balance body and mind, which will enable you to experience the clarity and beauty of your soul."

Some yoga practitioners teach that there are multiple kundalini energies in various parts of the body, which are active and do not require awakening. It derives its name from the focus on awakening kundalini energy through regular practice.

I did not know what any of this meant, and on the day of our Kundalini practice, our instructor tried to explain it to us in laymen's terms, but I still did not quite get it. What

I did know was that I had a feeling that whatever energy she was talking about tapping into soon would be released out of me, and it would not be pretty.

My **CORE**, the place within myself where I feel most connected to God, was also a place where I felt an enormous amount of trapped energy during the time of my yoga

Disease is a dis-ease.

teacher training. Call it trauma, anxiety, nervousness, pain, angst, or maybe just a shattered heart. I now understand that I was diseased (at dis-ease), by not dealing with the loss of my mom and my breasts. Disease is a dis-ease. I was not at ease with myself, and the Kundalini yoga practice we were about to begin together would show me that in a very raw and sickening way.

"Okay everyone, we will start in child's pose." Our instructor directed. "Please begin by tuning into your breath. Breathe in, breathe out. Now, go ahead and set your intention for class."

This was still a time in my life when I was always searching for any sign from my mother that she was finally at peace, so of course, my intention went there, to her.

"Mom, this practice is dedicated to you. I love you. I miss you every moment of every day. Please come to me to show me you're okay."

We began.

Our instructor took us through a pretty rigorous class, involving different postures and rapid breathing exercises, which included one called Rocking Bow pose with Lion's Breath.

We lay on our bellies, reaching back to grab onto our ankles, and arched our backs into what resembled a bow (or close enough). Next, we began slowly rocking back and forth, back, and forth until our Lion's Breath added in rhythm with our rocking bows.

"Okay, now stick your tongue out as far as possible and each time you rock back, inhale and when you rock forward, forcefully exhale." Our instructor encouraged, "That's it, that's it…now pick up your pace, you've got it!"

I am coachable, therefore I did as our instructor was coaching us to do until I began to feel somewhat nauseous, so I stopped. When I looked around, I noticed that others had stopped too. Our instructor was very good at reading the room, so she moved forward to close the practice and explained to us that the Rocking Bow pose may have been a bit more advanced for some, especially if you were not accustomed to backbends.

We finished with Savasana, my favorite part of any yoga practice. A time to simply relax. Every Friday together we always closed the day with a short practice and Savasana, and I usually fell asleep. Only this time, after the vigorous Kundalini, I felt an instant migraine coming on. Instead of envisioning my mother and trying to talk with her in another failed attempt, I spent my Savasana trying not to vomit.

Migraines are all too familiar to me because I grew up with them, and although now I experience them few and far between, I know when one is about to hit. There is no mistaking the signs. It starts above my right eye, and moves across my forehead, in a quick and violent intrusion of whatever I am trying to accomplish. A migraine has the potential to put me in bed for the rest of the day.

After class was excused, I didn't stay to linger about and talk with my classmates who have now become my friends. Instead, I rushed to my car so I could get home, make my room into the darkest cave possible, and crash into bed to try to sleep it off.

The next day, I woke to a migraine hangover. Meaning, still groggy and a bit queasy, but able to function. Despite the "hangover," it always feels like Christmas morning when I wake up from the excruciating pain that a migraine causes. Those of you who are unfortunate enough to experience these types of headaches know exactly the sweet relief I am talking about.

I began to rehash what the heck went wrong in the previous day's practice when I remembered that our Kundalini Instructor asked that we email her post-class to give feedback and ask any questions. I decided to pour myself a cup of coffee in order to nurse my migraine hangover before I sat down at my computer to check in with her.

"Hi there." I began my email. "Thanks again for a great practice yesterday. You are an amazing instructor! I do want to share with you what happened to me after class…"

I went on to tell her all about my migraine, how suddenly and forcefully it came on, and that I was just a little curious about this whole energy awakening thing. Like what in the actual hell did I do?

She kindly, and promptly responded, "Hi Valerie. I am so glad you enjoyed the class. You are all great yogis! I am so sorry to hear about your migraine. May I ask, is there anything going on in your personal life you would feel comfortable sharing? I ask because certain asanas (postures) and breathing exercises in this type of practice will unveil trauma, unbalanced, or trapped energy."

No, you don't say! I thought to myself as I read her email and began to feel another deep unsettling feeling in my **CORE**, realizing that whatever we did together in that practice was stirring up a whole mess of trapped crap inside of me. However, at that time, it was too much, too quick.

I thanked her for her loving response and decided to move on.

Baby steps down my path of resistance, I reminded myself, baby steps.

Our yoga teacher training curriculum moved on to meditation. *Ahhhh,* I silently thought to myself, *Now this is something I think I will really like and would also like to get better at.*

For years, on and off, I tried to meditate, but until my yoga teacher training, I never dedicated a set amount of time to this practice, to this discipline. Now with this new lease on life, a contract written in pencil that I had made with myself (pen was too permanent), I welcomed discipline.

Lara announced, "Okay class, today we will move on to the next part of our curriculum and learn about mediation. We will discuss what it is, and how to practice, which by the way, is a very personal practice and there is no right or wrong way, only suggestions I will share. Over the course of the next several weeks, I'd like for you to set a specific amount of time aside each day to meditate." She continued, "Please write in a journal, how long your meditation was, was it guided, was it to music or was it a silent meditation, etc. Together, we will share our personal experiences, but only if you want to share yours."

Okay, I said to myself. *Homework, we have homework. I like setting goals; this is goal setting. I have got this!*

I did not have this.

"Dear Diary" (aka, my Meditation Journal),

Today I waited until no one was home, set a timer on my iPhone, and silently tried to sit in quiet meditation for at least ten minutes. I made it to five, and they were not quiet minutes.

Next class, when it was my turn to share my experience, Lara asked me, "Valerie, what was popping in your mind as you were trying to quiet it?"

"Oh, I don't know, nothing important, random things I guess," I responded. "Things like, what I have to pick up at the grocery store, not to forget to write a note for Collin to get out of school early for a doctor appointment for tomorrow. Just things I have to get done, I suppose."

Lara smiled. "That is so common, I assure you. It happens to me, especially when I first started meditating. It just takes practice. If it helps, keep a notepad and pencil by your side next time. This way, when a random thought pops up, write it down and try to let that thought go. Remember, you may simply just come back to your breath. It is hard to quiet our minds and narrowing it down to just focusing on breathing in and out, may help."

All good things come to those who practice.

Practice. Practice, practice, practice. As a coach, I knew this: *All good things come to those who practice, right? I have got this!*

Nope. Still did not have it. Not even close.

On my second attempt with our meditation homework, I decided to set up the perfect atmosphere. I did all the things. All the things! I lit candles in my bedroom, played soft music, and sat upright with the perfect posture, looking like the cutest little Buddha on my bedroom floor.

It was quiet. I closed my eyes. I began breathing in through my nose and out through my mouth. *Remember,*

Valerie, you can always go back to simply focusing on your breath,
I reminded myself of what Lara said to me earlier in the day.

Monkey mind started out strong right out of the gate!
Oh no you don't! I said to my brain, but my brain kept insisting
on intruding. Determined, I stayed focused, concentrating
solely on my breathing.

It was working—I felt myself begin to soften, beginning
to drift in and out of a subtle dream-like state until…

"Mom, mom," Bailey and Collin came bursting into
my room, unaware that their mother was trying to be all
Zen-like. So, in a perfectly un-Zen manner, I responded,
**"WHAT?!! WHY CAN'T I TAKE FIVE MINUTES
TO MYSELF?!"**

"Sorry," Bailey apologized on behalf of both of them,
but Collin's face looked equally regrettable for interrupt-
ing whatever the hell was going on in my bedroom. Collin
asked cautiously, "We just wanted to know what time
dinner will be?"

"Dinner will be when I have reached my Zen, which
may be never, so we will all starve." I sarcastically responded
back to them.

Confused. Both of their faces look absolutely confused
by their mother, who was trying yet another method of
CORE-restoration for herself.

"Never mind," my response softened, "I'll explain later,
I have this meditation homework. Dinner is now, I'll start
dinner now."

"Dear Diary" (aka, my Meditation Journal),
Is the only way to find Zen, in the quiet? If so, I may never find it, or not until my children start cooking dinner for themselves or move out!

Just as before, class reconvened, and once again, we each shared our personal experiences with our meditation assignments. I frustratingly shared mine.

"Seriously, I can't find any peace and quiet in my house, and I've tried! I did all the things. I lit the candles, the finding a comfortable position like a Buddha thingamabob, I have tried it all."

"Why does it have to be in your home?" Lara asked.

"I'm not sure, I guess that's where I assumed it should be?"

Damn it! There's that word, showing her face in my vocabulary again, the word: should. Lara went on to confirm why I 86'd that word from my vocabulary.

"Remember Valerie, there is no right or wrong or any place it *should* be. This is part of the assignment, for you to discover what works for you. Soon, you will learn that meditation can be done anywhere, any place, at any time. In time, with practice, you will learn how to go within and without all the things, as you so put it. But for now, if you need a place inside of your home, where do you think that may be for you?"

Meditation can be done anywhere, any place, at any time.

"My closet," I answered her. "No one will bother me in my bedroom closet."

The next time I shared my experience with the meditation homework in class, which by the way, was a slightly better one, I earned the name, "The Closet Meditator!"

Throughout our meditation series, as promised, each time did improve for me (as most things do with practice). Some were longer and uninterrupted, although others were not. I found each session to be a lot like the physical exercise I was used to in that each one was different. There were days when I wanted to practice and other days when I forced myself to carve out the time, but each time I did, I never regretted it.

One evening practice in particular stands out.

It was a cold November night. I was waiting for my daughter to finish dance rehearsal, and I decided to wait in the car. It was lightly raining out, and I found myself becoming a little drowsy.

It is well known among family and friends that the car is my Kryptonite when it comes to keeping my energy up. I am not your girl if you want someone to sit shot gun to keep you company on long road trips—I will be fast asleep in no time, that is unless we agree on a good audio book or my playlist, of course.

While sitting alone in my car, waiting for Bailey to finish, I decided it was as good a time as any to meditate. Remembering what my teacher said about being able to meditate anywhere, at any time, I reclined my seat back and began to listen to the rain.

That night was one of the first times I truly began tuning inwards to tune out the stressors in my life.

There I was, in my car, unaware of my outward sur-roundings, noticing only the tempo of my breath and the steadiness of the raindrops, and both, before long, felt like they were one and the same. Rhythmically, like the waves of an ocean, placing me in a dream-like state of Nirvana that soon took over my body and quieted my mind, I felt myself beginning to dive below the murky surface of life. I felt myself going within.

There are no words to encompass what that experience was like, but I knew that it was something that I wanted to acquaint myself with again and again. The peace, the ease, the lack of dis-ease, was held within me for those few moments, which as it turns out, was forty Zen-like, heavenly minutes.

After that night, I added the practice of meditation into my tool kit as one of the items that I need to pick up and use in order to stay **CORE-strong.** Meditation has become part of my Spirituality practice as another form of prayer.

It has been many years since I earned my yoga teacher training certification and learned how to meditate. Since then, this closet, car, bedroom floor, waiting room, and yoga-mat meditator has developed her ability to be able to tune in to tune out all the things (or most anyhow) in her life that try their best to deplete her **CORE** or dim her light.

Like that young lady did to the punk in *Girls Just Want to Have Fun*, now when something isn't sitting right with me, I act so that I may be part of the solution that is right for me, especially when the solution is to just walk away. "To Thine Own Self Be True." True **CORE-restoration.**

"To Thine Own Self Be True." True CORE-restoration.

CORE-RELATIONS

(Questions to ask yourself)

❧ Has there been a time in your life when you have been
fearful of speaking up or sticking up for yourself?

_____

_____

_____

❧ How do you wish the situation were handled?

_____

_____

_____

❧ What is one skill that you have learned that has
helped you to tune out stressors in life and stay
grounded, stay calm?

_____

_____

_____

COREAGEOUS Challenge: I encourage you to carve out ten
minutes each day over the next three weeks dedicated to meditation practice. If meditation is not a new skill for you, try adding
a new type of meditation, breathing practice, etc., or try adding ten
more minutes to your current practice. For more information on
how to add meditation to your daily routine, along with additional

COREAGEOUS tips on living a heart-centered life, visit my website to sign-up and receive free emails: https://valeriejwalsh.com/ or hop on over to my Instagram: @valeriejwalshauthor

@VALERIEJWALSHAUTHOR

The goal is to become disciplined about this one item so that, soon enough, it becomes a healthy habit.

Share your progress on social media to help you stay account-able, using the hashtags: **#COREageous, #COREstrong,** and **#CORErestoration.** If you are more of a private person and prefer not to share online, write down your daily completion of this **COREAGEOUS Challenge** to help keep yourself on track and accountable.

CHAPTER THREE

SPIRITUAL QUEST

My Unindoctrinated
Union with God

IF YOU ASKED my seven-year-old self whether I would one day volunteer my time in the Catholic Church and become a Confraternity of Christian Doctrine (CCD) Teacher, I would have likely said, "no way in hell," I mean heck—no way in heck—because I would have **never** said hell. I was too scared of it.

I grew up in the 80s in East Syracuse, New York, and I was raised in the Catholic religion. I don't believe my experiences were much different than most young Catholic girls' experiences, but I will only speak for myself.

I remember having a lot of mixed feelings and thoughts about the organized religion I was indoctrinated into. Some wonderful feelings and memories included: love, happiness, belonging, fellowship, structure, excitement, validation, and friendship. Other not-so-wonderful feelings and memories included: fear, pressure, confusion, anger, shame, and boredom.

One of my earliest memories was a combination of both wonderful and not-so-wonderful feelings.

Saint Mary's Church, Minoa, New York.

I was seven years old, and it was time for our religious education class to make our First Holy Communion. Finally! This is the time when we would earn the most sacred right to eat the magical little wafer that the priest passes out during Holy Communion, but the BEST part, I remember thinking, *we would get to drink the wine!*

This made me feel excited and validated as a good Catholic girl. A wonderful feeling.

I recall thinking that this meant I was getting to do adult things, and THIS was important to me.

When it came time to rehearse how the ceremony would be conducted in our church, we started by finding out who our partners would be.

Mine would be Shawn.

Shawn was a lot taller than me, which (because of his sheer size) made him seem older. But Shawn was a gentle giant and a gentle soul.

This partnership made me feel happy because we were friends. A wonderful memory.

Our First Holy Communion rehearsals were led by a nun named, Sister Mary Catherine. I promise I did not make that up for the sake of storytelling, this was truly her good solid Catholic name. At birth, when given that name, she was destined to become the cliché scary-as-all-holy-you-know-what Catholic nun.

When Sister Mary Catherine began explaining what Holy Communion was, and the grand importance and sacredness of it to our faith, it went something like this:

"Boys and Girls, sit up straight. Sit up, I said, **SIT UP AND LISTEN!**" She commanded, and at once, we obliged. She scared me! She scared ALL of us! She was especially scary to a group of seven- and eight-year-old children!

She made me fearful of some of the leaders in our church. A not-so-wonderful feeling.

"The Holy Eucharist is the consecrated bread and drinking of consecrated wine—children, this **IS** the bread of life and the blood of Christ!" Sister Catherine proclaimed in her shaking, dictator-like, and intimidating manner.

This made me feel confused. I remember thinking, *What does consecrate even mean, and aren't we just eating bread? What happened to the little bread wafers I see the adults*

getting? Wait, is that real blood? I thought it was wine! ***I AM
NOT DRINKING THE BLOOD!!!*** *What is really happening
here?* I felt duped.

Why couldn't Sister Mary Catherine just keep it
simple, make it beautiful, and describe how special and
sacred this moment would be for all of us? Maybe she could
have used a metaphor to convey its beauty and meaning
and meet us on our level instead of trying to scare us
into believing.

She left me confused. A not-so-wonderful feeling.

From that point on, until I had my own children, I practiced
blind faith. I never questioned (at least not out loud) anything
that was taught to me by any of the religious leaders in my
church, even when my gut was telling me differently.

The wonderful memories and the positive influential
leaders of Saint Mary's Catholic Church (who truly impacted
my **CORE**) would later influence my decision to become
a religious education teacher for my own children.

Memories of my religious education teacher, Donna B.

Oh, Mrs. Butterfield, now that is a name that just
instantly gives me a warm and cozy feeling. I mean the
word butter is in her name, and who doesn't like butter?
It just came so naturally to love her and her heartwarm-
ing last name.

Donna had just begun teaching CCD when she first led our class. She was young, beautiful, approachable, funny, and enthusiastic about being our teacher and our friend. If you asked me to recall what specific lessons Mrs. B reviewed from the curriculum she was surely instructed to teach, I couldn't tell you.

What I can recall is not so much what she taught, but how she made all of us feel, which was loved, supported, heard, and special. Donna was an important person in my life. I wanted to be like Donna B when I taught my children and their friends.

Donna made me feel unconditionally loved. A wonderful feeling.

When major life decisions had to be made, Donna was always a trusted sounding board for her students. Like when a girlfriend of mine was contemplating if it was the right time for her and her boyfriend to have sex for the first time. Now, imagine, I believe we were about fifteen years old, sitting in our religious education class and gathering up the nerve to pull our teacher aside and ask her about sex.

"Mrs. B, may I talk with you privately after class today?" my friend nervously asked our teacher.

"Of course you can!" Mrs. B kindly assured her.

"Okay, thanks. Valerie is going to stay with me if that's okay, we both have some questions." My friend pulled me right in, but that was okay, we tended to do things in pairs like most teenage girls.

When class was over, my friend and I eagerly waited for everyone to leave. As soon as the room was empty, and only Mrs. B, my friend, and I were left, Mrs. B asked, "Okay, sweetie, what is it you wanted to ask me? Remember, you can ask me anything, and whatever you say here, stays here." Our teacher said warmly, and we both knew she meant every word.

My friend began, "Well, my boyfriend and I, we have been dating for over a year now, and we are thinking about doing it. You know...IT"

"You mean sex? You're thinking of having pre-marital sex?" Mrs. B asked, trying not to seem as surprised as we both knew she really was.

"Yes. We are talking about it," my friend answered, feeling a bit ashamed for asking. But Mrs. B quickly dissolved her shame by the gentle tone in her voice.

"Ummmm, well okay, okay, you know what our religion says about pre-marital sex, don't you? It teaches us that sexual love between a man and a woman is to be saved for marriage. That our flower is a gift for our husbands after marriage, and it is very special." Mrs. B explained, without judgment, only emanating pure love and kindness. However, my friend and I could not help but focus on the word that she chose to use in place of vagina—flower!

From that point on, whenever referencing our lady parts "down there," our vaginas became known as our flowers.

Our teenage years are a crucial time for personal growth. During a time when teenagers are exposed to many challenges, such as peer pressure and social influences, it is crucial to have a trusted leader in a young person's life to help them form a solid foundation for their future. This is what Donna Butterfield did for me. She was my safe space. She was someone who I could confide in and trust. Her leadership allowed me to explore my faith, ask questions, and seek wisdom without the fear of judgment.

Thank you, Mrs. Butterfield.

Another impactful leader who helped shape me into the woman I am today was my youth minister, Glenna Sobol.

Glenna was truly my spirit guide; she still is to this day.

This woman NEVER ran out of energy! She helped teach me about inclusion, nonjudgment, acceptance, love, respect, and forgiveness. Especially, how to forgive oneself. I grew up in a house full of addiction and undiagnosed mental illness, and I went to Glenna for so many different reasons over the years. She was my rock, my true north. Glenna was my soft place to land.

As our youth minister leader, Glenna was in charge of our youth group and all of the fundraisers, field trips, and retreats—let's just say she was in charge of most of the happy memories I have from growing up in the Catholic church.

When our youth group had overnight retreats, they were held at a local Catholic school (not a school I attended) that was used to host our religious education classes and events. Glenna would open these events up to ALL children— children of all faiths and religions, boys, and girls, you name it. Glenna would welcome them with open arms. She was a mother to all.

Glenna was no fool, and she knew exactly what she was doing. She wanted to create a **CORE-family**. A place for children to feel loved, happy, and safe. A place where children felt that they belonged. A place of fellowship and structure. She made it exciting and, in doing so, many lasting friendships were formed.

That is how you keep children, and adults alike, engaged—through support, acknowledgment, and by keeping the subject matter exciting.

Like the relationship I had and still have to this day with my non-blood-related brothers, Seth and Sean.

Seth and Sean grew up across the street from me in a suburb near Syracuse, New York. They were not related by blood either. Sean came from a very traditional Catholic family, while Seth came from a mixed faith of Catholicism and Judaism.

From kindergarten up until I was about fifteen years old (when my mother divorced her second husband, a person who is not worthy of the title "stepfather"), most days you could find me hanging with Seth and Sean after school. They were my boys, my peeps.

Sean and I attended the same religious education classes together, which left Seth out, not that he was losing any sleep over it. But when it came time for our retreats, Seth wanted to be a part of all of the fun, as he would hear about the awesome times his friends were having together in our youth group.

Before one particular retreat, Sean and I decided we would ask Glenna if Seth could come to our next weekend event.

While I don't remember the exact conversation we had with Glenna, I am sure her response went something like this:

"Well sure he can come! The more, the merrier! Just make sure that kid doesn't bring his BB gun or those snappers!" Two of the things Seth was famous for having and using to torture us, all in good fun, of course! Glenna knew him well enough to anticipate he may try his best to sneak those items into our retreat.

It was just like that with Glenna. The more, the merrier, and with that spunky attitude of hers, our youth group grew to be one of the largest and most active youth groups in all of Central New York.

These countless memories are just some of what I took with me when I made the decision to help my children and their friends grow in their faith.

I wanted to be like Glenna, one of my strongest spiritual guides.

Flash forward to my adult self, agreeing to become my children's religious education teacher.

During my time teaching religious classes for both of my children and their friends, I drew from the wonderful memories and feelings that both Donna Butterfield and Glenna Sobol gifted to me. That is all the way up until my son made his confirmation. I am not quite sure what these ladies would think about why I left the constraints of the Catholic church in order to grow my faith into what it is today, which is a very intimate and fluid practice—one that feels more authentic to me and true to my **CORE.**

During my years as a practicing Catholic, I often found myself questioning certain things the church not only frowned upon but condemned. I do not consider myself an activist in anything (for now), other than the importance of what we can do each day to protect our mental, physical, emotional, and spiritual health in order to live a life that is heart-centered. With that in mind, I will not list the many grievances I have with my former religion and its rules; instead, I will share one particular story as an example of why I have moved on and found a different way to practice my faith and continue to build my **CORE.**

It was the year before my son, Collin, would make his confirmation. Confirmation is one of seven sacraments in the Catholic church. It is a two-year program in which students begin the work to complete the third sacrament of initiation into the Catholic church, the first two being Baptism and First Holy Communion. Some believe that your Confirmation is one of the most important sacraments to make because it is where you make the decision, for yourself, to continue to be a practicing Catholic, instead of the decision being made for you, which is usually the case in Baptism and your First Holy Communion.

One of the lessons leading up to my class's Confirmation ceremony was about choosing to move forward in God's Grace, even in the toughest of circumstances.

It was a Wednesday afternoon, and like any good teacher, I was reading through my curriculum at the last minute. Truth be told, I always had good intentions of planning my lessons way ahead of time, but then, well, life.

As I was reading the material and making my notes in the margins, I jotted down, "How do we choose to move forward with grace, and what does that look like?" I looked up at the clock on the microwave in my kitchen. "Crap!" I said to myself, realizing I would be late to teach my 9:00 a.m. spinning class if I continued to focus on the lesson plan.

Quickly, I grabbed my bag and headed out to the gym, abandoning my planning for later.

I was forty-eight years old at that time and still taught a group exercise class that I was certified in almost thirty years ago. An era where exercise instructors made playlists on cassette tapes. I'd spend hours listening to the radio spinning

"Today's Top Forty Hits" off my Boom Box in order to catch the song I wanted to add to my workout mix. I was always at the ready to hit the play and pause buttons simultaneously to record. The time I spent making up playlists and routines never mattered because I had a passion for teaching exercise classes. A passion that still lives in me to this day and lights up my **CORE** in a way that is indescribable, maybe because it's such a pure feeling. It is tribal, wild, and immensely freeing. To exercise, sweat together, and fire up the endorphins that are needed for most people, especially me, to get through our days, is something I always look forward to.

After class was over, I headed out to go back home to my lesson planning, but before leaving the gym I bumped into Justin or J-Money, as he is more commonly known both at the gym and around our community.

"Heeeeey, what's up?" Justin said when he noticed me passing by the front desk and heading for the front door.

"Not much, how are you?" I asked.

"All good, just waiting to get out of work, I have fifteen more minutes, then I get to go home and chill," he replied while coming in for a hug. Classic J-money, always making time to say hello and giving a warm hug.

"I can wait fifteen more minutes for you to get out if you need a ride home; do you have a ride?" I asked.

You see, when Justin was ten years old, he was in a horrific car accident that left him with a traumatic brain injury, which prevents him from obtaining a driver's license. Most days he walks a VERY dangerous road to and from work. J-Money is one of the nicest people you'd ever want to meet; he is well-known in our town and just as well-loved. As a result, he doesn't have to walk for long because someone will usually drive by, notice him, stop, and turn around to offer him a ride to wherever he is going.

"That'd be great, Valerie. I'll be right out." He headed off to complete his checklist for his daily responsibilities as a facility team member.

While in the car, Justin asked me, "What are you doing for the rest of the day?"

"Oh, not much. I'm going home, a bit of laundry then I teach CCD later." I answered. I was quickly reminded of what the class lesson was focusing on: *choosing to move forward in God's Grace, even in the toughest of circumstances.*

Here I was, sitting next to someone who had done exactly that. Justin literally lives his life with more grace than most people I know. As I realized this moment was a Godsend—having Justin in my car and being given the opportunity to ask him to deliver God's message to my students—I asked:

"Hey J-Money, I have a question for you."

"What's sup?"

"Would you like to come speak to my CCD class later today?" I asked him with excitement at the possibility of bringing in a very inspirational person and using his story to drive home the lesson of choosing grace.

"Sure!" he said, without even quizzing me on what the lesson was about or what exactly he would be doing. That is Justin, living a life of service, of gratitude for the second chance at life that he was given.

I explained the message of the lesson and what I would like him to do: to tell his story, which could be as much or as little of it as he was comfortable sharing.

Without any hesitation, he agreed, and I let him know what time I would pick him up later that day.

When the time came for J-Money to speak, my class had already completed the curriculum, which included a written story, scenarios, and activities to help break down the overall lesson, but nothing would be more impactful than what they were about to hear. I could sense the excitement and anticipation in myself and within the room as everyone anxiously waited to hear this brave young man's poignant story.

"Okay class, I'd like to introduce you to my friend, Justin. I work with Justin at the gym, and some of you may know him already from around town." After introducing him, I took my seat, allowing Justin to walk up to the front of the classroom to speak.

Justin shared with the class that he was in a terrible accident when he was only ten years old while riding with his brother in a car driven by their mom. He explained that he sustained the worst of the injuries and had to be flown by a medical helicopter to a local hospital, where he remained in an induced coma for some time.

Justin said that when he woke up from his coma, he not only awakened with his physical life (albeit a new neurologically challenged one) but a renewed spiritual life as well. A spiritual life that included an immense gratitude that he was alive and a child of God. He explained that he currently had a feeling of purpose, which was to share his story and carry God's word for others to hear. Justin told the children, "I wake up every day and live my life for God."

As his colleague and friend, I could attest to all of what Justin was saying to my students.

The emotion that poured off Justin was palpable in our classroom.

The children and I continued to listen intently as he went on to explain that every single moment of every single day he makes a conscious effort to make God proud by the choices he makes in his life. From the friends he chooses to the way he exercises to respect the body God gave him, to the forgiveness he has given to his mother, who I can only imagine took much, much longer to forgive herself. As a mother, I found myself filling with deep empathy as Justin said this, and it was apparent to me how deeply Justin loved his mother, his family, himself, and above all, God.

Justin shared openly and honestly about not living his life in resentment or dwelling on the past. He explained, "If you choose to hold on to regrets, it will poison your spirit, your **CORE.**" He realized that if he chose to be angry and hate God for what happened to him—or blame anyone for the accident—he wouldn't be where he currently was, and he knew that God saved him for a reason.

If you choose to hold on to regrets, it will poison your spirit, your CORE.

"Today is a gift!" Justin declared to the kids. "It is a gift that I thank God for, each morning when I wake up, and every night before I go to sleep."

When Justin finished…

Radio silence.

Cautiously, I looked around the room to see how my students received his message. Not a single student was looking down at their lap trying to sneak a peek at their cell phone or distracted by anything whatsoever. Each one of my students was visibly moved. Some were moved to tears, while others displayed a look of pure admiration for the man who just shared his heart, his soul, so selflessly and so intimately.

Before sitting down, Justin left the kids with one more very important lesson.

Surround yourself with good people.

"Kids, I am serious, you've got one life, no regrets, be sure to surround yourself with good people."

Wow. Talk about impactful. Justin had just driven home a message that even the best of written materials could never have matched.

I have strong faith that angels walk among us, and Justin is a prime example of that by carrying out God's message of choosing love and grace even in the toughest of circumstances.

When class was over, I rushed home, full of adrenaline from such a moving experience. Without giving it much thought, I logged onto Facebook to share a picture of Justin and me that we took together when class was over.

The caption read:

 "When your eighth Grade CCD lesson is on grace and love, you bring in this guy to share his story. Nobody better, baby. Nobody. Love you, Justin."

The comments of support and love began to roll in. Each message was one of support and appreciation. Well, all except for one.

It was 10:30 p.m. My phone buzzed, alerting me of another text message. It was late, and normally by now I would have already put my phone up for the night, but the parents of some of the students were still texting me, blown away by what their kids came home to share with them. Apparently, some kids hardly waited until they got home, breaking down crying in their car at the impact Justin's story had on them.

However, this text was not from one of the parents, and it was far from kind or Christian-like in my opinion. In fact, it appeared to be quite an angry message from the head of the Religious Education Department at our church who, judging by the words she chose to type to me, was outraged that I brought Justin in to talk to the class.

IN ALL CAPS she blasted me:

> HOW COULD YOU INVITE SOMEONE TO COME SPEAK TO YOUR RELIGION CLASS WITHOUT RUNNING IT BY ME FIRST?"

She scolded me at the end of a not-thought-out rant that went on for one much-too-long paragraph of run-on sentences and accusations. You know those texts. The ones with the giant blue conversation bubble that nobody wants to read through in its entirety.

Unfortunately, I chose to read it and responded with, "You are out of town, and this was truly last minute, so I ran it by your assistant when I arrived to teach. I would hope that after over ten years of volunteering my time to lead CCD classes, you would trust my judgment before placing such harsh judgments on me."

She continued on and on by text. My phone alerts kept rolling in. "Ding…ding!" Exhausted, I silenced my phone, and tried my best to also silence my mind; instantly,

I regretted the decision to read her text right before I tried to fall asleep.

How could such a beautiful night turn so ugly so quickly? By poison, that's how. By dichotomous thinking, by people who can only see things in black or white. I am not certain if the Religious Education Director was upset by the lack of control over the decisions made while she was out of the office, or if it was years of pent-up resentment from her and me butting heads over various issues, but that was the last time I was willing to try to resolve our problems.

When others try to disrupt our spiritual health, we have to set boundaries.

When others try to disrupt our spiritual health, we have to set boundaries. On that night, my boundary was silencing my phone.

The next morning, I decided to email the Religious Education Director, along with her boss, our priest. But first, coffee. I find I am much more reasonable after coffee.

With my coffee in hand, I began my email, stating the facts of how Justin came to be invited to speak to the class, and I accepted responsibility for failing to ask permission. I wrote that I understood that the protocol was in place to protect our children. I asked the director to try to do her best not to view things so rigidly (as she seemed to be doing), and instead, look at the bigger picture of how impactful Justin's story was and how it drove home the lesson of God's love and grace. To perhaps open her heart to other resources, such as inspirational speakers, to come in and share their stories as Justin had, since it was incredibly impactful for the students.

I also requested that, from this point on, the director only communicate with me via email or in the presence of another person, such as her assistant or our priest, as this was not our first rodeo together, and apparently, we needed a rodeo clown. I made it clear that she was to no longer text me, something that I had allowed for far too long and would no longer willingly participate in. Neither the priest nor the director chose to respond to my email. I felt as though it was swept under the rug, which tended to be a familiar tact among some of the leaders I came across in certain churches.

That was the line in the sand for me. The line that was drawn in front of me, pushed me to make a choice to remain an active member of the Catholic Church or allow myself to cross over the proverbial line, toward a spiritual practice that would allow me to feel more connected to God.

I honored my commitment to see my final religious education class make their Confirmation. That was in 2022.

After finishing my time as a faith formation teacher, I have become more committed to my spiritual faith in ways that feel authentic to me. Today, my spiritual practice includes pieces of various religious traditions as well as spiritual methods. By choosing an approach that is suited for me, rather than indoctrinated into me, I feel more connected to God, to my higher power, than ever before. For me, faith is an action word. I try my very best to quite literally do the next right thing to make my Father, my God, proud. I try my best to grow and to protect the heart that he gave me. I am not perfect, none of us are, but I live with true intention to practice love and kindness, and to follow The Golden Rule of treating others how I would want to be treated. I believe each one of us is on this earth to make connections and to share our heart—our **CORE**—and that there are many different ways we may honor the purpose God has for each one of us.

Faith is an action word.

One of the prayers, or mantras if you will, I have written for myself:

> **"God, please lead me to people, places, and things that continue to bring me closer to you, to my purpose and truth, and ward off anything that doesn't."**

There will always be a special place in my heart and in my memories of the time I spent teaching religious education to the countless children I had the privilege of sharing time with. One of those wonderful memories was the time I wrote a poem for my elementary-aged religious education classes:

Our Forgiving Father

God loves you for
Who you are.
In his eyes,
you're as bright as the stars.

He is there to listen,
To whatever you say.
Nothing you could do,
Would make him walk away.

If you make a mistake,
And your heart feels a little sad,
Talk to God,
And I bet you'll be glad.

No one is perfect,
We all make mistakes.
But God's love is perfect,
And that's really great!

So try your best to live
In God's loving light.
Making good choices,
Doing what is right.

And remember one thing,
Remember who you are.
You're a child of God,
You're as bright as the stars.

Although I may not be a practicing Catholic any longer, I still hold on to many of its rituals and traditions as they offer structure, and I am a person who thrives on a certain amount of structure. Religious ceremonies and customs are a beautiful part of religion and one that I will continue to hold on to.

I love to pray, and although my prayers are less formal and now more of a conversation I have with God, they are no less important than the ones I used to recite in church. I also find that now I listen more to my heart and pray intentionally for the opportunity to recognize God's will for me. HIS, not mine. Sometimes this includes setting boundaries or even cutting off anyone or anything that weakens my **CORE**, the place within where I can go to feel God's presence, my conscious contact with God. I have learned that setting boundaries IS practicing love and kindness because holding on to something or someone as a response to outside pressure or programming is neither loving nor kind, even when it is based in religion.

Setting boundaries IS practicing love and kindness because holding on to something or someone as a response to outside pressure or programming is neither loving nor kind, even when it is based in religion.

CORE-strengthening lessons from my religious upbringing also helped to form the woman I am today.

In life, we will all suffer, and in the realm of religion, suffering holds a significant place in human existence.

Most religious practices have similar views when it comes to life and the inevitable suffering we will all face as humans. The belief is that suffering is built into the fabric of our existence for a purpose. I have experienced continuous, and sometimes brutal, lessons of what suffering may bring. Most practices teach that suffering provides individual spiritual tests, and the way in which we respond reveals a lot about us.

> *Suffering exists to test one's faith and has the power to unearth hidden parts of ourselves that we may not have known existed before.*

My experience has proven to me that statement is true. Yes, suffering is inevitable, and I do believe suffering exists to test one's faith and has the power to unearth hidden parts of ourselves that we may not have known existed before.

Each time I suffered; it taught me something as well. Below are three lessons I have learned from suffering.

Clarity

Life is busy. Most of us are too busy moving from one task to another and one day to the next; one week turns into a month, and before we know it, another year has gone by. That is, until something happens in our lives that has the force to make time stand still.

When suffering arrives at our doorstep, everything else seems to fade into the distance, except for the situation that is causing the suffering. Think about it. Have you ever been given bad news, and in the moment the news was being delivered, tunnel vision took over? Where every voice around you starts to sound like the teacher in Charlie Brown? I have. That is until I snapped back into reality, and the clarity of what was truly important rose to the top of my priorities.

I caused myself further suffering by drinking to dull the pain or enhance my mood. Ultimately, clarity is what I gained when I learned that only sobriety would help me find the peace I was searching for.

There is a beautiful prayer, often referenced in my recovery program. It is called the "Serenity Prayer."

Serenity Prayer

God, grant me the serenity to accept the things
I cannot change,

the courage to change the things I can, and the wisdom to
know the difference.

Suffering has the ability to remind us of what really matters in our lives. Our faith, our family, our actions, and our choices. It can put things into focus and prioritize where we spend both our time and our energy. It has the power to give us laser focus on what we ought to be concentrating on and what we need to let go of.

In my life, through my own suffering, I learned to reevaluate how I respond to events. If you are able to come out on the other side of pain after your spirit suffers and your heart is broken, you often gain a fresh new perspective. When the smoke clears, what is left is a simple, pure, and precise view of what really matters.

Endurance

When I think of suffering, and the ability to endure unimaginable circumstances, several stories of survival come to mind. I am drawn to books and movies about adventure, risk, and survival. I find them not only entertaining but also incredibly inspiring. No matter how far we have evolved from our ancestral past of hunting and gathering, we are still instinctually capable of enduring far more than we give ourselves credit for. Sometimes we just need to be reminded of this. Listening to, watching, or reading other peeps' stories of survival helps to keep my endurance of spirit (or as you all know by now, what I refer to as my **CORE**) strong. I like to surround myself with winners, even when I am commuting to work; I download inspiring stories of survival on Audible.

While there are many stories that fascinate me about the human spirit and what it is capable of when put to the test, I am usually more drawn to stories where external forces, like environment, disease, or injury, come into play. Except when involving children or pets—seriously, I cannot go there!

Recently, one of my favorite stories of survival, and the power of the human spirit, is the story of Hillary Allen. Hillary's story is the perfect example of how she was able not only to endure an unimaginable amount of physical pain but also emotional and spiritual suffering as well. She shares her story to show her readers the possibility of triumph over tragedy if you are willing to endure and do the work, which includes the willingness to be vulnerable and ask for help.

Hillary Allen is a world-class ultrarunner, among many other things. To me, she is a warrior, and yet, very relatable. In her memoir, *OUT AND BACK*, she writes about the time she fell 150 feet from an exposed cliff ridge on a mountain. During her fall, where she felt every single moment, she crashed and then was airborne again. She fractured her back and broke multiple ribs, both feet, and both of her lower arms. Her horrific accident caused her tremendous suffering. Hillary endured blows not only to her body and athletic career but also to her spirit, the **CORE** of who she was.

I related to so much of what Hillary shared about her suffering—how her accident took away so much of what her identity was tied to, which was her athletics. Not that I am a world-class athlete by any means, but much of who I am, and what makes my **CORE** light up, is tied to physical movement. Though not on a world-class level, I have coached and participated in countless running, endurance, and cycling races, as well as multiple individual and team events. When I went through my double mastectomy with reconstruction, the tools I counted on (outdoor exercise and endurance sports), in order to keep my spirits up, were taken away from me for some time. During that time, I could feel my sense of self, who I thought I was, slipping away from me. There were many times when I felt hopeless and lost.

Hillary shared so beautifully and candidly how, after her accident, she could feel herself falling into depression and a state of hopelessness. That is, until she remembered who the hell she was and decided she would fight and do the work that was necessary for her spirit to endure everything she would have to face. I appreciated how honest and vulnerable she was, especially when she wrote about how hard it was for her to ask for help. Hillary shared how important it was for her to rely on her community for support during her time of healing. This was something that also did not come naturally for me—asking others for help. It is a **COREAGEOUS** choice to reach out to friends, family, and your community in times of need. It is not a sign of weakness, but rather a testament to your strength and resilience.

Enduring the physical aftermath of a tragedy is hard, but my experience with suffering has proven that the true fight for endurance will be tested when trauma tries to steal who you are. When suffering tries to suffocate your spirit, you have to remember who you are, or at the very least, have the willingness to surround yourself with good peeps who will remind you of this.

Suffering gives all of us the opportunity to learn just how strong we are. It allows each one of us to discover the ability to make choices for ourselves to allow for better days ahead. These choices will lead us forward onto paths where we are meant to grow and endure more than we ever imagined we could.

Endurance is not just in sports; it is also in suffering.

Purpose

Last but certainly not least, suffering has revealed how to turn my pain into purpose.

Interviews of how prisoners of war survived years of torture, solitary confinement, and unspeakable suffering, reveal one common thread among them. Each survivor shared that they were able to go on another day because they kept their purpose at the forefront of their mind. Whether it was the hope that they would be released to get back to their family or another reason, their purpose drove their spirit to continue to move through their suffering.

Having a purpose in life is crucial for our well-being. It provides direction toward our goals and a sense of identity and fulfillment. It makes us feel like we belong, and are part of something, especially when we bring others along for the ride.

When I was a running coach, I would use my training acronym, **CORE**, as a tool to have my clients draw out their map toward their goals. This simple acronym helped to keep them purpose-driven.

CORE

C   Challenge (personal goal)

O   Obstacles (things standing in the way of your goal)

R   Reason (your why/your purpose)

E   Exercises (training plan)

Helping my clients to focus on their "why" or their purpose for their suffering (otherwise known as 5:30 a.m. training runs) was one way I would coach discipline over motivation. Keeping their **CORE** reasons at the forefront of their mind was a powerful coaching tool, and spiritual practice as well.

I never would have imagined that my suffering, specifically the tragedies I faced and wrote about in my first book, would eventually lead me to what God has in store for me.

Now, as an inspirational speaker, mental health advocate, and writer, I have discovered that my purpose is to share my experience, strength, and hope so others will know they are not alone. This has been an incredible gift, one that I am extremely grateful for with each opportunity that comes down my path.

I truly believe we all have the power of the Holy Spirit within us, and that holy spiritual purpose is carried throughout humanity in ways that are both known and unknown. Ways like suffering and discovering our purpose, after enduring hardships. Ways like making mistakes, learning from them, and sharing our experiences to give others hope that there are better days ahead as long as we have the willingness to try.

The most impactful lessons in our lives are often after weathering the storm of suffering.

Having faith, in whatever way our belief system has instilled in us, allows us to recognize we don't need to rely on just ourselves, and it is healthy to reach out for help. Our faith enables us to stay grounded in the love of God (or however you identify our higher power). That same faith reveals that each one of us is here on this earth to be of service to one another in some way, shape, or form. And it is that faith that prompts us to be kind, forgiving, patient, and non-judgmental because we are all suffering or will suffer at some point in our lives.

We all have a purpose, and some will discover it before having to go through suffering. I had to learn the hard way. I have learned the most impactful lessons in our lives are often after weathering the storm of suffering.

I believe that we are more alike than unalike. I believe that our spiritual connection to God is very personal, and organized religions are just one of the maps we may choose to pick up to find the path to our destination—a connection with God and living a life that is heart-centered.

Along the way, I have discovered that this woman of faith needs many different kinds of maps.

Like the CORE of an apple, we die a little more each time if we allow people, places, or things that feel like unauthentic practices within a religion to keep taking bites off of us.

At times, these maps still lead me to church, but they have also led me to temples and synagogues. I find the power of God and my spirituality in many areas, including music, hiking, conversations, service, recovery groups, reading, writing, biking, meditation, and of course prayer.

I also believe that, like the **CORE** of an apple, we die a little more each time if we allow people, places, or things that feel like unauthentic practices within a religion to keep taking bites off of us.

I know there is power in prayer.

 PRAYER. THERE WILL ALWAYS BE PRAYER.

My map includes a compass that is powered by prayer and meditation, pointing me toward **G**ood **O**rderly **D**irection (God).

CORE-RELATIONS

(Questions to ask yourself)

🖋 Are you holding onto any old, indoctrinated beliefs that are no longer serving you?

_____

_____

_____

🖋 Have you ever come across an angel who has walked into your life? If so, who was it, and how did they impact your faith in God, or God as you understand your higher power to be?

_____

_____

_____

🖋 In the space provided, write your own daily prayer, guided meditation, or mantra that helps you to live a more heart-centered life.

_____

_____

_____

COREAGEOUS Challenge: This may be a tough one, but I hope that you will give it a try. I encourage you to take a moment each day over the next three weeks to pray for your enemy. Enemy is a harsh word, and hopefully, you don't have any, but perhaps there is someone in your life who you are not gelling with. Maybe there is a manager or co-worker getting under your skin? Or, maybe a family member, someone in your life with whom you are frustrated or angry. The goal of this is to see if by praying for this particular person every day over the next three weeks, you begin to feel more at peace with them. This prayer is really for your spirit.

Share your progress on social media to help you stay accountable, using the hashtags: **#COREageous** and **#COREstrong**. If you are more of a private person and prefer not to share online, write down your daily completion of this **COREAGEOUS Challenge** to help keep yourself on track and accountable.

CHAPTER FOUR

86'D WORDS

The Three Words I Loathe

WORDS MATTER. SETTLE down, I am not talking about politically correct words here; I am referring to the three little words that have gotten under my skin. Those words are: Fine, Should, and Moist. Unlike an annoying sliver that comes on suddenly, that you must remove at once, these three little words worked their way under my skin, over time. They earned their place on my 86'd list by attaching themselves to situations or people who have stunted my growth. Whenever these three words are spewed out of someone's mouth, I feel like that same mouth is taking little bites out of my proverbial **CORE.**

In no particular order of offense, let's start with the word Fine.

Fine

My recovery group loves their acronyms, almost as much as they love their slogans. One of the acronyms they have for fine is:

> **F** Freaked Out
>
> **I** Insecure
>
> **N** Neurotic
>
> **E** Emotional

I know a lot of "fine" people, and I used to be one of them in one way or another. Fine people drink too much, smoke too much, clean too much, eat too much, spend too much, exercise too much, and so on. Fine people settle, instead of admitting the way they are really feeling. At least this has been most of my personal experience with this word.

Fine people settle, instead of admitting the way they are really feeling.

My mother was fine. Every single time you asked her how she was, she would tell you that. Never once would she dare reveal what was really going on in her life, in her head, or in her heart. Of course, she couldn't, she had been in survival mode since the day she began her adult life as a teenage mom. A circumstance that catapulted her into living a chaotic life. How would society respond to a mostly single mother, married at eighteen, mother of two daughters by nineteen, and divorced by twenty, only to remarry a sorry excuse for a husband and a stepfather to her girls? They would judge; at least that is what she convinced herself of. She also convinced herself that she was fine, and every day she adorned her fake fine mask for other people's benefit.

Keeping our troubles or our feelings from trusted loved ones in our lives is not good for our health or our relationships.

That is how this word has snuck its way into most of our interactions, with the intention of protecting others from what may really be going on in our lives, our heads, and our hearts. I am not insinuating that we are required to tell everyone about our private matters. However, keeping our troubles or our feelings from trusted loved ones in our lives is not good for our health or our relationships.

In my world, this word immediately has the power to make me believe that someone is holding back because for so long, it attached itself tightly to my mother's quivering lips. Lips that held back so much of what she really wanted to say, like it was their full-time job as some sort of gate keeper of her true feelings. Whenever my mother chose to use the word "fine" to answer any question that would have prompted such a curt, one-word response, I knew she was holding something back to protect my sister and me.

Verbal abuse. Emotional abuse. Alcohol abuse. Pill abuse. Depression. Anxiety. Shame. Remorse. All of these things, and more, are what my mother was experiencing when she claimed she was just fine.

Still to this day, the word lands with an impact on my heart, which is far removed from its intent. Instead of hearing that everything is really, truly okay, I hear, **"BACK OFF!"**

Fine is fake to me, even when uttered by the purest and kindest of people, who may only have good intentions.

> *The word "fine" is a crutch, a word to lean on, keeping people from what they really want to say.*

The word "fine" is a crutch, a word to lean on, keeping people from what they really want to say. Maybe they really want to answer, "I am freaking out, insecure, neurotic and emotional!"

Fine is a short and sweet word, just like me, or so most think. Seriously though, most days I am sweet, and that is because I am no longer willing to pretend everything is just fine if it's not. On the days that I am salty, so be it. I am human, and far from fine.

In the event you and I are ever to meet one another someday, and I ask you how you are, please know, I'd rather hear the other four-letter word come out of your mouth than the word "Fine."

Should we move on to my next 86'd word? See what I did there? Yes, I think we may just do that.

Should

"Should" is a loaded word. The Oxford English Dictionary defines it as, "indicating obligation, duty, or correctness, typically when criticizing someone's actions or yourself."

Really, I mean aren't we hard enough on ourselves without inviting a word like "should" into our daily vocabulary to remind us of all that we are not doing? Words are important, especially the ones we say to ourselves.

The word "should" is tied to expectations, and expectations are premeditated resentments, another little gem I have picked up along my path of resistance. The path that has led me further away from my default characteristics and vices (the comfort zone I'm tempted to fall back into). Vices like control are very easy to fall back on. As a mother, I often found myself telling my family what they should or should not be doing—I hope I at least do less of that today.

The word "should" is tied to expectations, and expectations are premeditated resentments.

When referring to expectations, I am not talking about goals or tasks. Expectations have a time and place, and

I believe they are to be set within a workplace. Expectations are a tricky thing to place on people, places, and things in our personal life. Communication is key when deciphering the differences among goals, tasks, or expectations.

Communication is key when deciphering the differences among goals, tasks, or expectations.

In the workplace, expectations are to be communicated clearly, and if they are not met, there will likely be consequences.

In our personal lives, instead of setting expectations, think of clearly stating what your desires or goals are with zero expectations of people, places, or things. In other words, be willing to accept what *is*.

For example, my full-time job requires me to travel. Not as a writer—contrary to widespread belief, most writers have full-time jobs. Writing is our passion, our art, and for most of us, not how we pay our bills.

Be willing to accept what is.

When I started to travel more, I could feel myself getting stressed out about all of the tasks that weren't getting done around the house, or at least not getting completed the way I thought they needed to be. So, I created a household checklist:

Try your best to keep up with these daily tasks, MOST especially when Mom is traveling.

⟍   Make your bed—and for the love of all that is holy—**PLEASE** check the foot of your bed for socks. I mean, who sleeps with socks on? **YOU KNOW WHO YOU ARE!**

⟍   Pickup your dirty laundry from the floor—**BONUS** for the one who starts a full load **AND** remembers to put it in the dryer.

⟍   Let's not get ahead of ourselves w/the next steps of folding said laundry.

⟍   Clean "your" bathroom—including all hair, toothpaste in the sink, and purple shampoo from the shower. The toilet—use your own discretion.

⟍   Dishwasher—it's magical!! Please use it. Hint...she also likes to be emptied.

⟍   Check grocery list—communicate as a team, add to list, and feel free to take a trip to the market.

⟍   Laundry—here we are again—it's never-ending, and neither is the task of me reminding you to **PUT YOURS AWAY!**

⟍   Vacuum as necessary—not a daily task, I'm not that cruel.

REMEMBER, IF YOU TAKE OUT THE TEAM IN TEAMWORK, IT'S JUST WORK, AND WHO WANTS THAT?

Feel free to borrow the list, it has become very popular among other families in my community, and I promise not to sue for copywrite infringement.

Now, if I lectured my family about all of the chores, they "should" be doing, they would immediately get defensive, at least I know that is how I would react. This one is not easy, i.e., accepting what *is*, and not how I think our home "should" be or "should" look. We control what we do not trust, and in doing so, we "should" everything and everyone to death.

\
We control what we do not trust.

The word "should" arouses feelings of guilt. Guilt that I am not doing something that I should be, instead of getting to do something that would be fulfilling and reaching the goals I have set for myself. This little guilt-loaded bitch of a word can easily be replaced, and I am on a personal campaign to replace it with the word "will."

\
The word "should" arouses feelings of guilt.

Try it with me for a moment and note how you feel when you say each sentence.

"I should go to the gym tomorrow."

"I will go to the gym tomorrow."

Feel the difference? I do, and you should too. Ahhhhh, I kid. But seriously, we should, I mean we *will* need to choose our words wisely if we are striving to feel more peaceful and empowered within our **CORE.**

I saved a light-hearted one, and likely the most universally loathed word for last. The word, moist.

Moist

I realize I am not writing any groundbreaking revelation here by admitting my disdain for the word moist. Really important scientists and researchers have conducted multiple studies to discover why so many people feel disgust when they hear this word. Like most writers, artists, and grown adults, I will tie this one back to my childhood trauma as well.

The trauma of the haunted and moi….okay, the moist basement of the old farmhouse I grew up in.

When my mother remarried that sorry excuse for a husband and stepfather, I was around five years old, and my sister was six. We moved from our small apartment into an old farmhouse with a dirt basement. This basement was, of course, haunted, or at least that is what my sister and I convinced ourselves of. It was haunted by the souls of the seven sisters who had lived in that house, and they all died there. That is how the story went—a story that was told to us by our asshole stepfather who thought it was funny to scare the crap out of us. This basement was also the place where our mother stored her potatoes and onions. I can still picture it, my mother standing in the kitchen, at the white porcelain sink, prepping dinner. She'd call out to one of us:

"Monica, Valerie, would one of you please run down to the basement and grab me four potatoes?" I imagine she was probably making Shepard's pie that night, one of the many staple meals that was her go-to, and also a popular choice during the 80s.

"It's your turn, I did it last time." Monica would say, protecting herself from the scary, haunted basement. "Besides, I am practicing my guitar."

I'd think to myself, *Anything to get away from hearing you play "Oh Mandy" by Barry Manilow on your Andy Gibb one more time!* The ghosts of the seven sisters were less scary than that!

I'd rush down the basement steps to the wire basket hanging overhead off of the beam full of spider webs, just out of reach. Standing up on my tippy toes, careful not to look left because we NEVER looked left or stepped any further than we had to, I'd grab what was needed for dinner. Man, how I wished we had a pantry in our kitchen.

Just as quickly as I ran down the basement steps, I ran back up, returning to my mother, completely out of breath.

"Here you go." I'd hand the four potatoes over to her, after all, it was the least I could do for a woman who worked all day and still made time to cook dinner from scratch for us most nights.

Each time I fetched something from the basement that held the souls of the seven sisters, it left me feeling cold and afraid, which is how I feel about the word moist. I feel cold toward it and afraid to use it in a sentence to describe anything.

Like me, this one is a work in progress. I may have to sprinkle the dreadful word in from time to time. I mean, how else am I supposed to describe delicious baked goods? "Hey kids, mom baked a nice clammy cake!" That won't work, that's just weird.

Damn you, Betty Crocker! Why did you have to program us to associate the word moist with your delectable desserts?!

CORE-RELATIONS

(Questions to ask yourself)

🖋 Are there any words that you would like to 86 from your vocabulary? Words that get under your skin and irritate you?

_____

_____

_____

🖋 What are your specific reasons for wanting to 86 these words?

_____

_____

_____

🖋 In the space provided, list your 86'd words along with the word you would like to replace them with.

_____

_____

_____

COREAGEOUS Challenge: I encourage you to identify one word that you would like to 86 and choose the word you would like to replace it with. The goal of this is to become disciplined about being intentional with the words that we say to others and to ourselves.

Share your progress on social media to help you stay account-able, using the hashtags: **#COREageous** and **#COREstrong.** If you are more of a private person and prefer not to share online, write down your completion of this **COREAGEOUS Challenge** to help keep yourself on track and accountable.

CHAPTER FIVE

CORE-PEEPS

Beautiful Friendships Are Like Beautiful Music

ONE NIGHT I was scrolling through Facebook when I came across a beautiful photo of a mother and child. They were part of the Himba African people. The photo had a caption underneath it that described a very special custom of their tribe. It read:

> The Himba people count the birth date of the children not from the day they are born or conceived but the day the mother decides to have the child.

When a Himba woman decides to have a child, she goes off and sits under a tree, by herself, and she listens until she can hear the song of the child who wants to come. After she's heard the song of this child; she comes back to the man who will be the child's father and teaches him the song. When they make love to physically conceive the child, they sing the song of the child as a way of inviting the child.

When she becomes pregnant, the mother teaches that child's song to the midwives and the old women of the village, so that when the child is born, the old women and the people gather around him/her and sing the child's song to welcome them. As the child grows up, the other villagers are taught the child's song. If the child falls or gets hurt, someone picks them up and sings their song. Or maybe when the child does something wonderful or goes through the rites of puberty, as a way of honoring this person, the people of the village sing his or her song.

In the Himba culture, there is one other occasion when the "child song" is sung to the Himba tribesperson. If a Himba tribesman or tribeswoman commits a crime or something that is against the Himba social norms, the villagers call him or her into the center of the village and the community forms a circle around him/her. Then they sing their birth song to them.

The Himba views correction not as a punishment, but as love and remembrance of identity. When you recognize your own song, you have no desire or need to do anything that would hurt another.

In marriage, the songs are sung together. And finally, when the Himba tribesperson is lying in their bed ready to die, all the villagers who know his or her song come and sing—for the last time—that person's song.

Ask yourself, who are your people? Who lifts you up when you are down and sings your song to you when you need to hear it most? We all have them: our peeps, our friends, our support system. Some may have a small group, while others may have a larger one. What matters most is the quality of your relationships versus the quantity. What is also important is your ability to recognize the peeps in your life who care enough about you and for you and your willingness to accept their support. If you

What matters most is the quality of your relationships versus the quantity.

haven't caught on by now, I like to call my people my **CORE-peeps**, or peeps for short.

Over the years and over the seasons of my life, my **CORE-peeps** have changed. Sometimes for the better, other times because, well, that is just the way life is. In my younger years, my peeps were my neighborhood and school friends. In my twenties and thirties, a few college friends (from my short time there). Eventually, I moved on to friends I met through work and also friends who were the parents of my kids' friends.

Now, in this current season of my life, my forties and fifties, my friends include various people who I have stayed in touch with from my previous seasons along with some very special **CORE-peeps**, who I have shared countless miles with biking, hiking, and running. All of these peeps are mixed in, old with the new, because that is what makes for a full and interesting life. A full life is one that includes relationships that are nurtured. Relationships that are worthy of the time and respect that is required to both build and grow them.

A full life is one that includes relationships that are nurtured. Relationships that are worthy of the time and respect that is required to both build and grow them.

My eclectic mix of peeps has blended together through the years, making for a beautiful symphony of friendships. Their symphony reminds me of a song we used to sing when I was a Girl Scout. It went like this:

Make new friends, but keep the old, one is silver and the other gold.

Make new friends, but keep the old, one is silver and the other gold.

My peeps are silver, gold, and a myriad of colorful personalities, each in their own unique way, and each with their own unique song.

There have been many times throughout my life when I needed my peeps to sing my song and my children's songs, too.

Like the time my daughter became seriously ill. Bailey was fifteen years old when she was diagnosed with stage three thyroid cancer. It was the same type of thyroid cancer that I was diagnosed with a short time after she was born, except hers was much further along. By the time Bailey's was discovered, it had metastasized into the lymph nodes in her neck.

The morning that Bailey woke up with a sore throat and a huge lump protruding from the front of her neck is still so vivid in my mind.

"Hey mom, mom…" Bailey called for me, waking slowly while making her way out of her bedroom to find me. "I don't feel so good. My throat is killing me, it feels like it is on fire! And… what's this? Look, I have this HUGE lump on my neck." I felt my heart fall instantly into my stomach.

I tried my best not to let my mind go to the worst-case scenario, but the truth is, once you have experienced cancer in your family, your mind tends to go there.

I immediately called her pediatrician to get Bailey in for the first available appointment.

Upon arrival at the doctor's office, the receptionist checked us in and immediately sent us both back to the examining room, where we waited a short time for the doctor. Not even long enough to play our usual game of "Eye Spy With My Little Eye," to pass the time.

When Bailey's doctor conducted his examination, he did not hesitate to take action. He had careful consideration for our family history, specifically my thyroid cancer and the possibility of a genetic connection at play in our case.

"I want Bailey to go straight to the hospital for an ultrasound, I'll have our receptionist set it up for you. As soon as I get those results, I'll be in touch." I could sense by the serious tone in his voice that this was no ordinary sore throat.

Bailey's ultrasound results led to a biopsy, and that biopsy led our family straight into one of the scariest times in our lives. My fifteen-year-old daughter endured a nine-hour surgery called a radical neck dissection. In this surgery, they removed her entire thyroid, the huge cancerous nodule that we spotted protruding from her neck, and numerous lymph nodes where the cancer had spread the tentacles of its disease. That biopsy resulted in a hypertrophic scar (thick red raised scar) across the front of Bailey's entire neck. That biopsy led to trauma, trauma that is not mine to write about, trauma that is hers, and still ebbs and flows within her to this very day. It is a good thing my girl comes from solid stock who know their worth. Though she may be a work in progress, aren't we all?

With Bailey's permission, I will share one particular story about the fallout from cancer. No, cancer is not always pink ribbons, fundraisers, and casseroles, especially when you are a teenage girl who just wants to fit in and feel comfortable in her own skin—a task that is already almost impossible, by virtue of just being a teenage girl.

Once Bailey was able to return to school, a sophomore in high school at the time of her illness, she tried her best to resume most of her previous activities and the responsibilities she had before her diagnosis. One of those included being a runner during her study hall. A runner was a person who would run errands for the front office. Errands such as bringing students their forgotten lunch from home or homework that was left behind, along with any other important messages.

It was an ordinary Wednesday, or as ordinary as a day can be for a person after their family has been stricken with a crisis such as cancer. I was working at the gym, training a client. Both kids were at school, and my husband, Brian, was at work.

During my personal training session with a long-time client, my cell phone buzzed. I did not usually have my cell phone on hand when working with someone, but my clientele knew a bit about what our family was navigating, so they understood. I needed to be reachable, should my daughter need me. Bailey was now experiencing panic attacks and severe anxiety—far from a pink ribbon, THIS is what cancer does to a person.

"Bailey, what is it? Are you okay?" I asked her, even though I knew that since she was calling me during her school day, she was not okay. We would soon discover it would be a long time before she would be okay again.

"Mom, please come pick me up, **PLEASE!**" She begged me.

As her mother, I tried my best to navigate when to bail her out and when to have her tough it out. This responsibility as a parent was brutally hard. There were so many times I wanted to just keep her home and protect her from the harsh fallout of this disease. We could stream continuous mindless series on the television while eating ice cream and snuggling. We could bury the hard stuff underneath fuzzy blankets that would keep us safe and warm. But then, there is life, and nevertheless, life goes on, even through the hard stuff. Life is not easy, and it is not our job as parents to make sure our kids never experience pain or how to deal with people's shit.

Life is not easy, and it is not our job as parents to make sure our kids never experience pain or how to deal with people's shit.

But on this particular day, this was more than just shit. This was pure evil. Evil spewed from a horrible senior girl, straight at my daughter—who was doing HER a favor.

Bailey continued through her tears, "Mom, I had to deliver papers into this classroom. After I handed the papers to this girl, I heard this other girl sitting next to her ask what happened to my neck. She told her, 'Oh you didn't hear?

That's where she tried to hang herself, but she failed!' And they both laughed at me! Please come get me now, PLEASE!"

WTF?!!! WTF?!!! WTF?!!! Ran on repeat through my mind; I was unable to think clearly and enraged with mama-bear emotions—emotions that are instinctual and wild in a moment like this, where all a mother wants to do is protect her child who has just been wounded by an animal—emotions that made me feel like I wanted to bust straight into Bailey's high school, grab that evil girl by her neck, and leave her, too, with a scar for people to question.

However, I am not my emotions. I am a mother and usually pretty sensible. So, instead, I made the responsible choice to reign both my emotions and claws in, so as not to be arrested for kicking a teenage girl's ass.

With my mama-bear claws retracted, I hung up the phone and reassured Bailey that I was on my way.

Ugliness.

That is one of the things cancer has the ability to bring out of others, pure ugliness.

While the disease itself, may leave the person battling it with scars that are visible, it may also leave a person with scars that cannot be seen by others. Scars that have the power to seep their venom into one's **CORE**, if allowed to strike. Whether it be venom spewed from a heartless teenage girl, from late-night internet searches by a scared teenage girl losing sleep over things she is too young to have to face, or venom from the pure toxicity of trauma, all of it is poison. All of it was spewed at my daughter during one of the most vulnerable times in her life.

Thankfully, cancer also has the power to gather your **CORE-peeps** in unison, to sing your song and repair your broken heart. Often, where there is great pain, there is also tremendous joy.

Joy is what we felt the day we returned from the hospital with Bailey after she recovered from her nine-hour operation.

Often, where there is great pain, there is also tremendous joy.

As we drove into our neighborhood, up the one-mile hill leading to our home, we began to hear Bailey's song. It was written on poster boards, held by her **CORE-peeps,** and it sounded like this:

> You've got this, B!

> You will dance again!

> You are beautiful, you are strong!

> Kick cancer, like a dancer!

> We love you, Bailey!

Her song was carried by her dance friends and their parents, as well as her dance instructors. It was also sung by her high school teachers, her guidance counselor, my friends, our neighbors, and our local community.

Bailey's song was carried emphatically by so many who were willing to share their happy songs when all she could hear was sadness. They sang until finally, one day, she was able to feel her beautiful song within her **CORE** once again. THIS is what love is, what humanity is. Humanity is lifting one another up, especially when someone is not in a place in their life to do so for themselves.

Humanity is lifting one another up, especially when someone is not in a place in their life to do so for themselves.

My son also has his own unique song.

Collin's song is carried by his **CORE-peeps,** as well as mine. Those peeps are the parents of whatever sport he is playing. When he was little, the baseball parents sang it. Today, it is sung by the parents of the cross-country team, track and field runners, his coaches, and the band of brothers on his running team.

When I have to travel for work, it results in times when I miss out on seeing Collin run. It is very hard, and I am probably the hardest on myself when it comes to not being present for one of his races. When this happens, I call on my **CORE-peeps** to begin to sing Collin's song.

His song usually begins with a group text message to the mothers of some of the runners on his high school team, and it goes a little something like this:

"Hey ladies, it's Valerie. I have a work trip next Tuesday and unfortunately, I will miss their race. Will one of you please keep me posted?"

Then, the singing begins.

"Of course, I'll text you updates" one **CORE-mama** replies.

"I'll try to video Collin running and send it to you" answers another.

"Don't worry, Valerie. We will cheer Collin on for you!" another reassures me.

That is how his song begins, and then it plays on. It continues through the cheers of the **CORE-parents** who sing Collin's song with sincere intention of love and support, as if he were their own. In the times when I cannot physically be there to sing for him, they combine their voices together to make up for my famously loud adulations! These peeps are the best and most humble group of parents that Brian and I have been blessed to have spent so much time with during our son's high school days. I will miss this experience and all of them dearly when this season of life is over. With each running event that passes, collectively we know that we are one step closer to becoming empty nesters and moving on to another season of our lives. Because of this awareness, there is an unspoken bond, and love among all of the parents, realizing we will never get these precious days back. Unspoken, except during the moments I decide to speak up to ensure everyone knows I am NOT going to be okay when our kids graduate and this is all over—that I will need each of them to belt out my song VERY loudly in order to drown out my tears.

Though the next season of my life will be so different without my children in our home, my past experience with change has proven to me that we will all be okay. Life will move on to the next season and symphony for all of us. However, this particular symphony that I am currently listening to and vibing in, may play on repeat in my head from time to time. It will be a familiar song, bringing wonderful memories with it each time I decide to get lost in its melody.

Move a muscle, change a thought, and surround yourself with the right people who have the vibrational power to lift you up, especially when you need them the most.

There are times in our lives when we may feel like we cannot hear our song anymore. Heartbreaking times where stress, depression, loss, trauma, overwhelming situations, and so on, have the power to drown our song out. When that happens, I have learned that all I need to do is change the station and listen to a different set of **CORE-peeps** singing for me, singing for one another. In other words, move a muscle, change a thought, and surround yourself with the right people who have the vibrational power to lift you up, especially when you need them the most.

In life, we will win, and we will fail. We will please, and we will disappoint. We will learn, and we will grow. We will love, and we will be loved. We will gain, and we will lose. And if we are lucky enough, we will do all of these things, surrounded by beautiful people and beautiful music. Music is such a special gift to each of us. Music has a way of amplifying what is in our hearts, where spoken words may fall short.

Music has a way of amplifying what is in our hearts, where spoken words may fall short.

May we have no shortage of both: good music and friendships.

CORE-RELATIONS

(Questions to ask yourself)

✎ Who are your **CORE-peeps**? Who lifts you up when you are down?

_____

_____

_____

✎ Was there a time in your life when you needed to lean on your support system? If so, what was the situation and how did your peeps support you?

_____

_____

_____

✎ In the space provided, write a song that you would sing for yourself, or one you would like another peep to sing for you.

_____

_____

_____

COREAGEOUS Challenge: I encourage you to find time each day over the next week, to let one of your **CORE-peeps** know how special they are to you. Make this simple and attainable. Maybe acknowledge them with a text or share a song that reminds you of them. The goal of this is to remind ourselves how important it is to let someone know that they matter and that they are doing a good job; it's as simple as that.

Share your love for this one on social media using the hashtags: **#COREageous**, **#COREstrong,** and **#COREpeeps.** If you are more of a private person and prefer not to share online, write down your daily completion of this **COREAGEOUS Challenge** to help keep yourself on track and accountable.

CHAPTER SIX

EXTROVERTED INTROVERT

Host Then Ghost...
Please Come Over, but Leave
by Six O'clock

PLACE ME ON a spinning bike in front of a room full of riders, or in the front of any group fitness class, leading the choreographed sequences of exercises for a room full of my gym peeps, and I am in my element. An element that gives me immense joy and fuels the fire in my **CORE**. In fact, the more people I am surrounded by in this particular element, the better and more energized I become. That is, until I am ready to go back to the peaceful solitude of my alone time. I need it to refuel. You see, I am a little bit of both extrovert and introvert. The atmosphere I am in, and the peeps I am surrounded by, will dictate which one.

In places where I feed off of the energy of other people—places like gyms, my workplace, events where I am volunteering or presenting, or anywhere there is teamwork involved—I am "on." I am the one raising her hand to read at my continuing education seminars. I am the one to volunteer to lead a group when there are breakout sessions during workshops. I am usually the leader or manager of most group settings. Believe it or not, I am also the organizer of most of the gatherings among my friend groups. In fact, I am usually the host.

However, I am also the one who likes to host, then ghost. I will be the first one to pull the old "Irish Goodbye" and sneak out so that I may retreat back to my introverted self before I become fully depleted by being in places that are too peopley. It's not because I don't like people, I love people! At the same time, I very much enjoy time to myself. I need time to shut down. Time when I'm not engaging with others.

I am your typical Extroverted Introvert.

You probably know a lot of us. In fact, maybe some of what I am saying is ringing true for you.

In my best Infomercial Narrating Voice:

> *Do you find yourself wanting to be around a lot of peeps in certain situations, but only becoming close with a few?*
>
> *Do you want to be both invited and not invited to certain events?*
>
> *In your free time, do you sometimes like spending it with others, but also enjoy spending time with yourself?*
>
> *Then you too, just may be an Extroverted Introvert, and we have just the prescription for you!*

Well, not literally a prescription, but I am willing to share what has been helpful for me to manage both sides of my personality.

Knowing what situations give energy and what situations take our energy away is important. Most people operate out of obligation, which is okay to some extent. We all have commitments and people to show up for, and that is the right thing to do. For example, as a sober woman, I am committed to show up for my brothers and sisters in sobriety, just as they have done for me. With my friends' milestones, such as birthdays, weddings, anniversaries, and other various celebrations where there is likely going to be alcohol and partying, I still want to be present for them. I have no desire to isolate myself from people who enjoy drinking, and I hold zero judgment about it. My choice not to drink, and the awareness of the boundaries that I have set for myself to protect my sobriety and energy, have kept my Extroverted

Knowing what situations give energy and what situations take our energy away is important.

Introverted head screwed on straight. Little tricks like showing up a bit late, so as to avoid the social anxiety that small talk may sometimes bring on, and leaving early, aka the "Irish Goodbye," are two of the ways I protect both my sobriety and energy.

Also, I understand first-hand the importance of avoiding isolation.

When it came time to arrange the details of my mother's funeral, we started collecting pictures of her life. My sister Monica, My Aunt Donna, and I carefully selected pictures of happier times. As we placed the photos onto the various poster boards, what I saw was a glaring timeline—as the years passed, my mother started isolating more and more. The further she fell into the trap of her isolative ways, the more affected she became by her mental illnesses.

> *Making meaningful relationships and avoiding isolation is a simple and vital way that we can protect our mental health.*

Now, as a mental health advocate, that is one of the items I speak to most frequently. Making meaningful relationships and avoiding isolation is a simple and vital way that we can protect our mental health, and I am passionate about sharing this tip, and many other practical ones, with as many peeps as I can.

Another thing that has helped this Extroverted Introvert is knowing who I am and embracing it. I have gained this confidence over time. Be kind to yourself if you are not there yet. Life has a way of awarding you with confidence, but only if you're willing to do the work that is necessary to earn it.

> *Life has a way of awarding you with confidence, but only if you're willing to do the work that is necessary to earn it.*

A few years ago, I was interviewing for a position that had opened up in my full-time profession. The job I was interviewing for was in a highly competitive field, where there were more candidates than job openings. The organization I was meeting with was well-known and male-dominated.

My interview was in New Jersey, inside a large corporate building, where this particular organization had arranged to rent a conference room in order to conduct all of their in-person meetings. This meeting was one of the final steps in the many stages of their interviewing process. Leading up to it, I had already submitted a video, conducted a personality test, gone through a few Zoom sessions, and spoken with their recruiter many times over the phone. Finally, I was given the opportunity to meet, face-to-face, with the upper echelon of this particular account.

I walked into the boardroom, where I was immediately met by their Executive Assistant. With formality in his voice, he greeted me, "Good morning, Valerie. It is so nice to meet you. Thank you for coming down here to meet with all of us today. Please, have a seat." He gestured for me to be seated at the head of a large oval-shaped conference table where a bottle of water was placed for me. Seated around the opposite side of the table, were six very professionally dressed men, all looking straight at me, in anticipation of asking the questions each one had prepared for me. I was prepared with the ones I had for them as well. Together, we shared the common goal of wanting to get to know one another a little more, in an effort to see if I was the right fit for this account, and if this account was the right fit for me. Instinctively, I knew this could not be done by placing me at the head of a cold conference table, a great distance away from where each executive chose to take their place. With that, I chose to take my place, as well as what move I would make next.

"Thank you, it's nice to meet you as well, thank you all for having me." I replied to the Executive Assistant; I looked over toward the others, picked up the water bottle that was placed down for me, and proceeded to ask the executives in the room, "Do you mind if I move a little closer to where you are all seated? Because THIS isn't intimidating at all!"

It just came out, and there was no taking it back—the honesty about the arrangement of the conference room and the sarcastic humor, which I often reach for in order to calm my nerves while trying to be sure everyone is comfortable.

Luckily, it was well received. They all laughed and invited me to sit a bit closer, and we began what turned out to be a very successful meeting.

Knowing who I am, and what I need, has always proven to serve me well. Yes, I may have social anxiety, but I have also learned how to work with it and manage it. Honesty and humor are great practices for managing an anxious mind and having to manage my social anxiety has also given me great emotional intelligence. While I may be an outgoing, high-energy, and strong leader, I also realize that I need certain things, like alone time, to recharge. Alone time is okay and necessary for me, as I don't let too many days of isolation string together.

Honesty and humor are great practices for managing an anxious mind.

Being a little of both is a good thing. On certain subjects, like exercise and mental health advocacy, I am a strong public speaker, this is my extroverted side. Other times, when someone is telling a story or needs to vent, I am a very good listener. I enjoy learning about other people and hearing their stories, as well as people-watching and observing. This is my introverted nature. I like being a part of a team and consider myself a good team member, as an extrovert. But as an introvert, I thrive while working independently, prioritizing tasks, and checking to-do's off of my list. It is no surprise that most writers are introverts and most often communicate better through writing than verbal communication. But my goal as a writer is to share stories of inspiration, and this requires me to draw from my extroverted side. My passion for sharing how to stay in strong physical, mental, and spiritual health requires a huge amount of my extroverted side to come forward when engaging in book events, workshops, seminars, and inspirational public speaking events.

Being a little bit of both is kinda like a Half-Moon cookie, for this Central New York native gal, known as a Black and White cookie to others. What I am trying to say is, that being a little bit of both can be a delicious and beautiful harmony when you learn how to balance it. Some days I'm a little vanilla, and others, a bit more chocolate. Mostly, I am just me, and I refuse to put a label on that.

CORE-RELATIONS

(Questions to ask yourself)

❧ Are you an extrovert, introvert, or a little bit of both?

_____

_____

_____

❧ What environments give you energy and fill your heart?

_____

_____

_____

❧ What environments deplete your energy?

_____

_____

_____

COREAGEOUS Challenge: I encourage you to take one of the tips that you shared from the question above and practice this tip daily over the next three weeks. Be sure your tip is simple and attainable. The goal of this is to become disciplined about this one item so that soon enough, it becomes a healthy habit.

Share your progress on social media to help you stay accountable, using the hashtags: **#COREageous** and **#COREstrong.** If you are more of a private person and prefer not to share online, write down your daily completion of this **COREAGEOUS Challenge** to help keep yourself on track and accountable.

CHAPTER SEVEN

COREAGEOUS CULTURE

COREAGEOUS Vibe and Together We'll Thrive

WHO SETS THE tone, the atmosphere, in your life? What vibe do you thrive in?

Our behavior will be impacted by tone, or what is today known as the popular phenomenon of culture. Whether we are talking about the home, the workplace, a sports team, or a school system, creating a culture of strong leadership, supportive relationships, and clear standards is key to achieving the goals being set by your team of peeps and the most important factor in driving their behavior is the culture that is provided. Bottom line, great results are driven by great behavior.

The importance of culture has become a topic of discussion for me personally, both at work and at home. The reason for this is that, as I write this book, I am one year into a new job where I am thriving as a result of the culture the company has provided. At home, this subject has become more prominent since my son is about to decide which D1 school he will attend. The culture of the team, the coach, and the university will play an important role in Collin's decision-making.

Before culture was a thing, good humans with good hearts were probably already working toward creating a positive and productive culture in whatever space or organization they were a part of. It has been my experience that all great leaders are ones that are encouraging. And, encouraging leaders are the ones who give from their heart, making them **COREAGEOUS** leaders.

What is a **COREAGEOUS** leader? It is someone who encourages another to be the best version of themselves by leading from their heart center—someone who is strong in their convictions and not just concepts. What's the difference? Convictions are heart-driven beliefs, whereas concepts (or mission statements) are just posters on the wall. Not that concepts and mission statements aren't important, they are. However, it is the culture that will drive the behavior of its people to work hard toward collective concepts and missions.

COREAGEOUS, heart-centered leaders understand the importance of providing a vibe where peeps may thrive.

Long before calling employees a "team" versus "staff," the words "team members" (when referring to my colleagues) just naturally rolled off of my coach tongue. I suppose that was my sports background coming into play when I took my first management job. There were not forty modules of computer slides to train me to call my team a team versus staff, probably because I managed a large multi-purpose gym; therefore, it wasn't a far stretch for me to use this terminology. It came organically. The key difference between staff and team is that a team accomplishes the work together, while a staff member accomplishes the work in any manner they see fit. In other words, team members collaborate toward a journey, while staff members are just doing a job. And we all know that journeys are fun, but jobs are work!

In other words, team members collaborate toward a journey, while staff members are just doing a job.

Leading teams is something I enjoy, and I believe it is one of my strengths. Understanding and caring about what motivates and empowers a team is a key factor of effective leadership. During my time as the assistant general manager of that large multipurpose gym, I loved my team of peeps—mostly. I tried my best to respect and understand, at least on some level, those who were a bit

Understanding and caring about what motivates and empowers a team is a key factor of effective leadership.

more difficult to love. Love being the key word here. While we may not always like everyone, always try your best to lead with love and respect.

To me, it's not rocket science. Lead with clarity, respect, and support from the heart, and you will be creating an effective culture that enables your team members to possess the confidence, self-worth, and self-esteem to do their jobs not only efficiently, but also with passion.

While we may not always like everyone, always try your best to lead with love and respect.

Providing a psychologically safe environment is part of creating an effective culture that drives great results. Numerous studies support the premise that a workplace/ environment that recognizes the importance of psychological safety as key to unlocking their team's potential results in greater productivity.

Pathways to successful workplaces (ones that create positive cultures that include psychological safety) will vary a bit in their methods—and in the ways they deliver these messages within their organization. Larger companies that provide modules for training their employees using a self-guided method for employees to navigate their way through the organization's cultural standards do so out of necessity to streamline processes. Large organizations need to make the training available to all of their employees, and there is nothing wrong with this style. However, taking it a step further, the successful organizations that put leaders into place to carry out the company's cultural message will put **CORE-**, heart-centered leaders into place who will work in person within their teams to further their development. Everyone will reap the benefits of keeping this type of vibe as a priority, one that is psychologically safe.

This is an important reminder of the importance of face-time, not Facetime. Body language makes a difference, and so often misunderstandings happen when communication is limited to email or online meetings. In a society where working remotely is becoming the norm, we need to find that balance. There are certainly pros and cons with each, and I am not going to tackle this complex subject here, but I will point out that I personally find it much easier to communicate in person than on a computer screen. The value of creating bonds from collaborating with a team member at work cannot be recreated by working remotely, or at least not in the same way. You can't shake someone's hand, fist bump, or high five through the screen of a computer.

In my experience, being part of both small and large organizations in everything from entry-level to management positions, to higher levels, the most successful companies have all walked similar pathways to reach their goals. That path must be led by action, and not just by words written down for training material or mission statements framed on a wall. Convictions over concepts win every time.

Any grouping of people will perform to the tone that is set by their leader. We have all heard the term, "success starts at the top," and while that is true, it is sustained by the peeps throughout the organization. The culture, tone, or "vibe" that is demonstrated by people in leadership roles, will have direct impact on a group's behavior, and therefore, drive what end results are achieved.

In a nutshell, culture is set by **COREAGEOUS** leaders who lead from their heart, and it is carried out by the team members they surround themselves with. These leaders take time to let their team members know they are valued and appreciated by communicating this often, and not just at their annual review.

Let's break down how to build a **COREAGOUS Culture** into three **CORE-nerstones** that work toward fostering a positive, productive, and psychologically safe and effective culture.

TRUST, VALUES, AND ATTITUDES

CORE-NERSTONE №1
Trust

Trust comes before everything else when working toward an effective culture so that is why we are talking about this **CORE-nerstone** first. In an environment where trust is fostered, team members are more likely to thrive, collaborate, and contribute the very best of themselves.

Think about a time you were in a meeting or a situation where you were afraid to be yourself, to ask a question or even admit to a mistake. Now think about the environment you were in. Was it one where you felt like you were being judged, or made to feel undervalued or less than? Was it within a workplace, sports team, or classroom where you felt like your mistakes were held against you? If you answered yes to any of those questions, then how could any trust have been built? It couldn't. Trust is earned, and easily broken. That is why it is essential for everyone to consistently build trust with small and diligent steps, each and every day. It is also important for leaders to be the greatest example of how trust is earned. It is a leader's job to encourage and push their team members to continue to grow. Team members' growth is in direct proportion to the amount of trust they have in their leaders.

> *Team members' growth is in direct proportion to the amount of trust they have in their leaders.*

Effective leaders will find ways to connect to their team members on not just a professional level, but a personal one as well, by listening, caring, and getting to know their colleagues. This connection also helps leaders to identify team members' personalities and determine how to manage them. Connection and building trust on a personal level helps to recognize an individual's strengths and apply them within the workplace. Most importantly, building trust on a personal level also helps to build a strong community and one people want to be a part of.

Strong leaders also help to build trust among their team when they are willing to be vulnerable by admitting to their own mistakes, owning up to them, and moving forward. Mistakes are just feedback. There are far too many people in leadership roles who are, or at least think they are correct, but who are also highly ineffective. Trust is the foundational **CORE-nerstone** of a positive, productive, and psychologically safe and effective culture.

CORE-NERSTONE №2
Values

I define values as the things that we choose to prioritize as important. You may also think of values as your beliefs or convictions. Our chosen values will guide our decisions and have a direct impact on our team, our peeps. With my training clients, I referred to our priorities as our **CORE-values.**

For example, when the gym that I managed first opened, one of my responsibilities was to do all of the interviewing and hiring alongside my friend and owner of the facility, Eric, better known to many as, E-Roc.

E-Roc and I both realized that when it came time to hire our personal training team, finding qualified candidates would be very challenging—well, qualified on paper at least. We lived in an area where there was not a huge pool of certified personal trainers. With that obstacle in our way, we hired based on personality, convictions, and overall energy. This was something Eric and I, as leaders, both valued more than any certification. We knew we could provide the required training, but personality and energy are something that usually cannot be trained. Frankly, you either have a "it" or you don't. The "it" we were looking for was a team of peeps who would vibe with the energy we were striving to create. Carefully, we selected candidates who had a positive attitude, patience, eagerness, and high energy about them. Together, E-Roc and I brought a wonderful team of personal trainers and group fitness instructors on, who all worked hard to make the gym more than just a place to lift things up and put them down. We created a community.

CORE-NERSTONE №3
Attitude

It really boils down to the way we think and feel—our response to both our personal and work lives. The way a person feels about how they are being treated can and will directly affect their attitude and performance.

Within a home, if a family member does not feel respected or valued, that will have an impact on how they participate (or not) within their family. As a mother, I know all too well how hard it can be to rally the troops to do their chores. If I allowed someone else's lack of immediate action to impact my attitude each day, I would spend most of my days pretty disappointed. Look, we are all human and operate in our own human ways and paces. Often, I have to remind myself to avoid placing expectations on people, as that leads to resentment. People are all different and move at their own pace, some are slower than others and procrastinate, while others like to get their tasks out of the way. As a mom, I try my best to set a tone of appreciation for a job well done, even when it is at a snail's pace! Trust me when I say, this is easier said than done, but I try my best to demonstrate patience and acceptance for solid effort. Set the tone, be the leader, and do your best to try to understand where someone is coming from. At the end of the day, as long as everyone is trying their best to do their part to make our household run, it's all good in our hood!

Within a workplace, If a team member does not feel appreciated or positive about their role, if a student does not feel acknowledged at school, or if an athlete does not feel valued as a team player, they will simply not work as hard for their team of peeps. If someone feels stifled from contributing enough or does not feel that what they are contributing is being recognized, they will stop trying. People want to know that what they are doing matters and that their contributions are important. I am sure you are familiar with the saying, "A person who feels appreciated will always do more than expected." Bottom line, this is a true statement. Team members will have an attitude of gratitude for their leaders and teammates when they feel respected and appreciated for their individual roles. It doesn't have to be grand; it is in the little things. When leaders touch base and check in with their team members on how they are doing, by providing feedback or offering flexibility and understanding, they are working toward boosting the overall attitudes within their team.

Team members will have an attitude of gratitude for their leaders and teammates when they feel respected and appreciated for their individual roles.

At the same time, we must take responsibility for our own attitude. If our response to a person or a situation is based on other people or situations in our life, we are setting ourselves up for a lifelong poor attitude. Even when there is obvious evidence that others are not doing their part, or have done something directly to disappoint you, only YOU can choose how you will show up and respond. It is easier to fall into the blame trap and complain, and it is much harder to make the choice to accept circumstances for what they are and adjust your response in a more positive and productive way. But the really cool thing is, having a positive and productive attitude and being mindful of our responses allows us to move past things we cannot control much more quickly than if we choose to respond negatively.

The three **CORE-nerstones**: Trust, Values, and Attitudes, all work together to provide a positive, productive, and psychologically safe and effective culture. Only when this vibe is set, are you ready to thrive and work toward your goals.

Goals are important and help push us forward by creating opportunities to put all three of the above **CORE-nerstones** into action. Your team's target, or bottom line, needs to be clearly stated, with a direction and a plan of action, but don't forget to trust and enjoy the process toward reaching your goals.

My recent experience watching Collin on his school's cross-country team demonstrates the importance of individual and team goals. (Added bonus: I love shedding some light on why cross-country running is, in fact, a team sport whenever I have the opportunity to do so.)

Although it is true that, as a runner, you run a race by yourself, you do not run it *for* yourself. Yes, you are the one putting one foot in front of the other, but all of the training and strategizing that takes place behind the scenes, before the actual race day, is what makes cross-country a team sport that has both individual and team goals. One of the biggest secrets to the success of a running team is the social component of being on a team with a positive culture and camaraderie.

Running is hard and relying solely on a written training plan to help keep you driven to meet your goals is not a smart plan. There are days when I know my son, Collin, has momentarily lost his ability to tap into his motivation, and he has to remind himself of the discipline within, as well as the overall team goals they have set together. Times where he must rely on his fellow runners for accountability and their collective energy to get him out of the front door and onto the dirt to run.

Currently, I am collecting photographs of memories to put together in a book for Collin to take to college. I am convinced that when he graduates high school if anyone should ask what his happiest days were, his answer will likely begin or end with a memory that includes a group of friends and fellow runners and their common goal of gathering together and pushing one another to be their very best.

Goals. They are important no doubt. However, the time spent reaching for our goals is about more than just an end result. All of the grit, sweat, time, energy, focus, failure, triumph, laughter, tears, lessons, and memories matter more than a single achievement.

Think about a time you achieved a particular goal, big or small. Now, try to remember—how did you feel after you achieved your goal, and how long did all of those wonderful feelings last? Was it months? Weeks? Days? The point is, the end result, good or bad, is fleeting. It is the person you become while striving toward your goals that matters. Our **CORE** purpose in life isn't to hit one goal after another out of the park. Our purpose is to set goals and take note of all of the lessons we learn along the way, especially the lessons we learn when we fall short.

It is the person you become while striving toward your goals that matters.

At the end of the day, I know as a parent, watching my kids achieve their goals is fun! I think we can all agree that winning is, in fact, fun. However, I hope my kids will always value the lessons they learned from the measures taken toward their goals and know that they are so much more than just an end result.

In the workplace, people are searching for more than a job, they want a journey toward something greater. By providing a culture where people may thrive, they may not always hit every goal, but they will certainly enjoy the journey along the way.

You may do everything correctly, and the outcome may still not turn out to be what you wanted for yourself or your team of peeps.

Acceptance of what is must come into practice and be prioritized in order to be resilient.

This is where acceptance of what *is* must come into practice and be prioritized in order to be resilient.

I see this with my kids, and it breaks my heart. Knowing that the lesson of acceptance is usually learned over time, through trial-and-error, it doesn't make it any easier to witness my children's crushing disappointment with an undesired outcome. Acceptance is hard. Especially when a person has done all of the right things and given their very best toward whatever goal they wanted to achieve, only to fail, or at least in their eyes, not reach the achievement they desired.

What if we could take the pressure off of the end goal? The fleeting moment of a medal placed around our necks, or a sales number and ranking listed on the white board that will only be erased in order to set next month's goals. What if we replaced the end goal with an overall acceptance of all of the lessons and moments that led to it? What if we were just proud of what we gained along the way while working toward our goal? Acceptance has the power to replace momentary happiness with enduring peace and productivity. Acceptance allows us to be resilient. It allows us to continuously learn and grow.

Acceptance has the power to replace momentary happiness with enduring peace and productivity.

Arthur Rubinstein, one of our most highly regarded pianists of all time, says, "Of course, there is no formula for success except, perhaps, an unconditional acceptance of life and what it brings."

Imagine how much more resilient we would be if we learned how to appreciate our efforts and passion more than the end result. Truth is, we cannot control what the outcome will be. There are too many factors both known and unknown, that can get in the way of an outcome we want for ourselves or our team. The willingness to accept the outcome has the power to be part of the beauty of life and the unpredictable nature of it.

I believe developing the habit of looking at whatever the outcome may be with an acceptance mindset (not a defeatist one) is key to moving forward on a path of resilience, peace, and productivity. In other words, if we want a different outcome next time, we need to let go of what *is* in order to move forward with the next right step.

Acceptance is a choice. A habit we all have the opportunity to learn with both time and practice.

Acceptance of others is also important in order to create a positive and productive culture.

It is of huge value for team members to understand and accept what each person does for their job; some corporations or workplaces call it cross-training. Now I am not saying that everyone will comprehend the details, have the skill set, or possess the requirements to do each job under the roof of one particular place, whether we are talking about in the home, school, workplace, or on a sports team, but at the very least, if we all understand what each person is required to do for their particular job, we will cultivate respect and understanding for one another.

COREAGEOUS leaders who help to foster **COREAGEOUS** cultures are gems. I am lucky to have been led by and inspired by some of the greatest.

One of my first **COREAGEOUS** leaders was the general manager of the health club where I first started my fitness career. Her name was Doreen.

It was the early 90s. A time of scrunchies, body suits, leg warmers, step classes, and the mixed tapes I made my spinning class playlists on. Aside from teaching classes, I also worked at the front desk at this particular multi-purpose gym where, at the time, Doreen was the general manager.

Doreen was a striking woman, with jet-black hair who was always styled beautifully. She dressed in business attire, not gym attire. She was a "Queen" as the kids say today. "Okay, Queen!" would have probably been my response when Doreen walked through the front doors of the gym, promptly at 9:00 a.m., ready to take on the day. Making boss moves in her chic business suit was her style, and no one stood in her way.

During her time as our leader, Doreen was creating a team culture before it was labeled as such. Each month, our individual departments would meet with their direct managers, but it was the quarterly meetings, with the entire team of over fifty employees, that everyone really looked forward to. They included a bit of cross-training with other departments. The goal was to understand the responsibilities of each department and individual to build respect for one another and encourage acceptance of each other as valuable team members. These meetings also included a bit of fun, which is why we looked forward to each new quarter.

Doreen would organize ice-breakers for team members to get to know one another a little bit more, as many of us were shift employees and had little opportunity to work with different people. She had us play a variety of team-building games as well.

We played games like Minefield. Random objects would be placed around the room, and we would partner up, one person blindfolded, and the other directing their partner from one side of the room to the other, without stepping on the objects. The objective, of course, was to build communication and trust.

Another one I remember playing was called The Human Knot. We would break off into groups of six to eight people; our small groups would circle up, raise our right hand into the air, and grab someone's hand from across our circle. Then, we would do the same with our left hand until we were all knotted up. A timer was set, and we had to work together to untangle our Human Knot. The fastest group won. This was another great way to urge employees to communicate and cooperate, and honestly, just to have a little fun and laugh at ourselves!

Activities like these helped to prepare our team for the not-so-fun days, because that again, is life.

When I think about the many influential leaders in my life, Doreen ranks right up there. It isn't because she was always easy on me, or a push-over—most great leaders aren't. In fact, most great leaders make decisions that we may dislike.

If I asked you who is one of your greatest influences, what would your answer be? I bet most people would answer a parent, a teacher, a coach, a manager, or a religious leader.

There is one thing all of the people listed above have in common if they have impacted your life. They have all lived a life of service. They have all sacrificed their own needs for the greater good of the team or organization, even if that meant one of their team members may become temporarily upset with them from time to time. A true leader will not always be liked. While that is not always a fair price to pay, it is certainly a worthwhile one.

Ask yourself, were you always happy with your parent(s), manager, coach, or teacher? If you're being honest, probably not. I know I definitely wasn't happy with the number of times I was grounded as a child for breaking my mother's rules, or when Doreen made certain calls as our manager that I did not necessarily agree with at the time. But one thing I did love and appreciate about my mother, Doreen, and all of the influential leaders in my life was that they held me accountable. They made me feel appreciated. Above all, I trusted them and therefore responded well when they pushed me to be the best version of myself and to grow.

My sister, Monica, is someone I have always looked up to as a **COREAGEOUS** leader who creates an amazing vibe for her team of peeps. When I took on my first role as a manager, the one as the assistant general manager at that large multi-purpose gym, Monica had already been in management for decades. In her role, she is extremely well respected. She excels at leading her teams, as well as supporting the leadership within her workplace. As adults, my sister and I have always lived in separated states, but I would often see (via her social media, such as LinkedIn) the various ways she would honor her teams and show her love and respect for them. Monica never forgets to acknowledge a birthday, work anniversary, or important milestone such as reaching a team goal. She is phenomenal at what she does, and because of her gift as a strong leader, and the skill sets she has learned along the way, her team of peeps produce great results for their organization.

With my sister as someone I could look up to, and with my own coaching style, I jumped at the opportunity I was given to lead a team of about fifty employees, consisting of facility maintenance, front desk, group exercise instructors, and personal trainers. I understood the importance of creating an atmosphere where the entire team felt appreciated and heard, and above all, worked to gain and maintain their trust. In doing so, we all worked together to get the job done, whatever it entailed.

Today, although I no longer manage that large gym, I still carry all of the leadership skills and traits I have learned along the way. Presently, I am still in a work environment that continues to align with what I value and look for in a healthy work culture. Whether I am a leader or member of a team, or just for myself personally, I always want to remain coachable—to grow by learning from others. I will always look for cultures that cultivate a vibe I want to thrive in and surround myself with great people along the way!

It makes me so proud to see that the importance of a positive and productive team culture has trickled down to my children and continues to be an important topic of discussion in our family.

My daughter, Bailey, works as an assistant manager at a dual-diagnosis home for people with mental illness and addiction. She shares with me all of her ideas about how to create an atmosphere of growth, not only for herself and her colleagues but for her clients as well. Whether she knows it or not, what she is creating is a team culture and she is a natural at it with her beautiful heart and mind. I am certain her company also has the forty-computer module slides to train this into her, but as her mother, I know it was built into her DNA.

My son, Collin, is currently a senior in high school. His accomplishments in both academics and running, have led him into the recruiting process for division one universities. One night, he was on the phone with a head coach from one particular college, when I overheard him say, "May I ask you a question? Who is your biggest inspiration as a coach; who is your mentor?" I knew what he was really asking. Collin wanted to know what their team's culture was about. He wanted to know if this running coach would be more of a Ted Lasso or Alberto Salazar type. It made me so proud to know that Collin valued the importance of the culture that was being created, and not just how many conferences or titles the team has earned. The fact that he is looking for a team to run for that will not only make him a better runner, but also a better human, makes my heart full.

COREAGEOUS Cultures cannot be left to chance. **COREAGEOUS** leaders and team members must work together to create the vibe in which they may thrive.

When this culture is created, it must also be protected. In doing so, homes become warmer and more loving sanctuaries, workplaces become more productive and supportive spaces, sports teams become stronger and better teams, and classrooms become more inclusive and safer. But before we can create this big picture, this beautiful culture to live in, we must first practice diligence in the small steps each and every day to create the culture we want, within the spaces we are a part of.

Now go out and be a Ted Lasso or be the most coachable member of a team a coach could ever dream of. I promise if you do, you will be the real winner in this game of life.

CORE-RELATIONS

(Questions to ask yourself)

❦ Name a time in your life when you felt part of a positive and productive team culture.

_____

_____

_____

❦ What was your role in helping to create this positive and productive team culture?

_____

_____

_____

❦ In the space provided, write down what you look for in the culture of any group or organization you choose to be a part of.

_____

_____

_____

COREAGEOUS Challenge: If you are a leader, I encourage you to find one way you can improve your skills to become a stronger and heart-centered leader. For example, participate in an online leadership course or take advantage of company-provided training. If you are not in a place of leadership yet, or even if that is just not your thing, I still encourage you to try out a leadership or growth mindset course for yourself. These courses provide useful information and skill sets that we can all benefit from. Many can be found online or locally through your library, colleges, or community centers.

Share your progress on social media to help you stay accountable, using the hashtags: **#COREageous** and **#COREstrong.** If you are more of a private person and prefer not to share online, write down your completion of this **COREAGEOUS Challenge** to help keep yourself on track and accountable.

CHAPTER EIGHT

REMAINING CURIOUS

The Importance of Remaining Curious, Coachable, and Passionate

I AM A huge fan of the award-winning dramedy streaming on Apple TV, *Ted Lasso*. If you are not familiar with this gem of a series, let me fill you in on its delightfulness.

Ted Lasso is about an American football coach who is hired to manage a British soccer team. He knows nothing about the sport, other than the fact that the British call soccer football, and football, as an American sport, is much different than the sport he was hired to coach. What coach Lasso lacks in the knowledge of the game of soccer, he makes up for in his undying enthusiasm, optimism, and determination. This show also reacquainted me with my love of all things buttery, such as the biscuits Ted shares in an effort to connect to his new boss, Rebecca.

One of my favorite episodes from Ted Lasso was in season one. There is a remarkable scene where Ted joins Rebecca for a drink at a local pub (Rebecca is the owner of the AFC Richmond football team that Ted is newly coaching). While there, Rebecca's cheating ex-husband, Rupert, walks into the pub with his new and much younger, fiancé. Ted plays darts next to Rupert, and before long, they begin wagering. If Ted wins, the deal is that Rupert can't go anywhere near the owner's box at the stadium while Rebecca is in charge. Ted wants to protect his boss from further emotional damage at the hands of her slimy ex-husband.

The game begins, and Rupert takes out his fancy, personalized darts, starting the game off strong, while simultaneously spewing criticism at Rebecca for every decision she has made since she took over ownership of Richmond. Ted sits back, ready to make his move. You see, before their game of darts began, Rupert had made assumptions about Ted, underestimating his ability to win.

Then, Ted shares one of my favorite quotes by Walt Whitman (something he is notorious for doing—giving life lessons through famous quotes and sharing a story to back the quotes up).

"Be curious, not judgmental," Ted softly states, while confidently holding his final dart, before throwing it and hitting a bullseye for the win. He continues to tell a story about how guys underestimated him his entire life, instead of asking questions to learn more, and how this experience in his life changed his way of thinking. If you watch the show, you soon discover Coach Lasso is curious about everything and holds zero judgment.

Powerful questions can come from a place of curiosity and not judgment.

The point of the impactful monologue given by the character, Coach Lasso, is to remind us that powerful questions can come from a place of curiosity and not judgment, and above all, to …

NEVER LET ANYONE UNDERESTIMATE YOU, INCLUDING YOURSELF.

His bullseye was not just on the dart board, but also in the game of life. Just imagine how much better our world would be if Ted Lasso ruled it.

Hey, a girl can dream. While I may not have the power to change the world, I do have the choice to remain curious and refrain from judgment.

Somewhere along the way in my life, I had a momentary lapse of both curiosity and judgment—curiosity in learning and growing, while placing harsh judgment on myself.

As early as I can remember, as far as academic memories of school are concerned, one of my favorite subjects was writing. Starting in the first grade, I remember our teacher introducing us to the subject of creative writing. We were each given a journal to begin our exploration into writing, with simple instructions of making an entry each day about anything we wanted to write about. From that point on, as the years progressed, so did my writing skills and passion for the subject. By the time I reached the fourth grade, my teacher took notice of my writing ability and suggested I be placed into enrichment classes for both reading and writing.

I remember feeling very excited about this opportunity, likely because someone noticed me and encouraged me, something I remember craving deeply growing up.

I loved being a part of the enrichment reading and writing group of kids. We were a small group of children, whose talents were being enhanced, and the sole focus was on our individual and collective skills. I recall this small part of my day being the only time when I felt comfortable in school—where I felt smart, like I belonged—and where I was thriving. I also recall when we had to return to our larger classes, and I would immediately shut right back down. I would not ask questions and found my attention span diminishing in the larger classroom setting.

While I cannot say for sure where or when I lost my curiosity as a student, my report cards reveal that it was probably around the age of twelve or thirteen, right around seventh grade. Middle-School Me lost her curiosity and confidence, and no one seemed to notice, not even me.

Middle-School Me was three years away from receiving the news that my mother would be divorcing her sorry excuse of a second husband. Middle-School Me would see her beautiful mother's light start to further dim. In those three years, her mother's light would quickly fade with the discovery that her husband, who constantly—and brutally—verbally abused her (and on occasion, also physically abused her) was now also cheating on her. Middle-School Me was trying to keep her head above the water and dodge the waves of chaos that were now crashing down upon her family. Middle-School Me was lost and confused. And Middle-School Me was also just three years away from taking her first drink.

I know now that I completely lost all of my curiosity around the age of fifteen, an age when I became more interested in partying than anything of true value. While I may have had moments of productive curiosity peek through, overall, I lost my purpose and passion the moment I looked for something outside of my true self—my soul, my **CORE**—to make me feel validated. Alcohol and binge drinking at parties to fit in stunted my spiritual growth.

While there is no single reason that teenagers experiment with drugs, or in my case, alcohol, Sober Me now knows there were many reasons that I began to binge drink, and for a long time, played it off as just partying and my right of passage. Reasons that included escaping, fitting in, and rebelling, as well as feelings of anxiety, neglect, and loss. As a teenage girl, it was a way for me to get noticed, a cry for help at a time in my life when I felt so confused and unsettled. Above all, I believe my binge drinking started for many different reasons, and they all led to dulling my curiosity and my passion.

While I do not regret my past, and I am a firm believer that the only mistakes we make are the ones we don't learn from, I still get sad for my younger self from time to time. But mostly, I like to use my time and my experience in a good way and not dwell on my past. It has become my passion to write and speak about the importance of having a purpose and to remain curious about the ways to live a heart-centered life.

> *The only mistakes we make are the ones we don't learn from.*

Speaking to younger audiences, especially middle and high schoolers, about the importance of remaining curious in order to discover their purpose and their various passions, has been one of the many gifts I have been given as a result of sharing my personal story. I feel strongly about reaching younger kids, so they may have relatable information about how the choices they make will impact their futures. I share with them that if they make a choice that is not right for them, that is a mistake, but they are more than their mistakes and deserve a beautiful, bright, purpose-driven, passionate, and curious future.

Our brains are highly vulnerable during adolescence, and early intervention combined with supportive and positive environments are key. Today, we are dealing with a healthcare crisis that still includes alcohol abuse, along with far more serious killers that encompass a wide variety of substances.

Opioid prescription drugs and the rise in overdose deaths, largely due to the powerful synthetic opioid fentanyl, continues its heartbreaking trend of being the biggest drug issue in America. It is killing our loved ones, more specifically, men ages thirty to fifty. One factor that leads to a higher risk of overdose in later years is trauma rooted in childhood experiences. That is why prevention is key. Talking to teens and young adults about the importance of finding purpose and passion, while remaining curious, is part of the prevention work that is needed. Gone are the days of "experimenting" with drugs and alcohol, as my generation did. Today, fentanyl—with its power that is up to fifty times stronger than heroin and one hundred times stronger than morphine—has the ability to kill the first time it is mistakenly ingested. Illicitly manufactured fentanyl is available on the drug market in different forms, including liquid and powder, and it is commonly mixed with drugs like heroin, cocaine, and methamphetamine.

In powder form, fentanyl is being made into pills that resemble other prescription medications. These fentanyl-laced pills are extremely dangerous, and many people may be unaware that the pill they are about to pop could be laced with this devil in disguise. Unless a drug is prescribed by a licensed medical professional and dispensed by a legitimate pharmacy, you cannot know if it is fake or legitimate.

In liquid form, fentanyl may be found in nasal sprays, eye drops, and dropped onto paper or in small candies, however accidental death by ingesting food/candy that has been laced is very rare.

According to recent studies, over 150 people die every single day due to synthetic opioids such as fentanyl.

You cannot see, taste, or smell this devil in disguise. Inexpensive test strips are available and can mean the difference between life and death. Naloxone, more commonly known as Narcan, is a life-saving medication that can reverse the effects of opioid overdose, is also available, and given out freely in many areas. Both of these items have unfortunately been criticized for the possibility of encouraging illegal drug use, but the statistics point to the opposite.

If you didn't know before, I hope you will realize the crisis we are in and will consider having both of these life-saving items on hand. Whether or not a person has accidentally ingested fentanyl or taken a drug intentionally, I will carry Naloxone with me, in the event I have to use it. It is not my place to decide who deserves to be saved, and the fact that some still have this point of view, honestly, sickens me. Naloxone is available in all fifty states. Most local pharmacies will distribute Naloxone without a prescription or go to www.naloxoneforall.org for more information on obtaining it.

As I am writing this, we are in the year 2023, and more synthetic drugs are being manufactured every single day. Our war is far from over, and while it is far too complex for me to fully understand how to stop it, what I do know is we can all do our part. My part has been early intervention and speaking with young people about the importance of finding their passion and remaining curious about it, as well as being open to opportunities to learn and grow. Early intervention is key, and helping children realize their potential, their purpose, and the curiosity to find their different passions in life is one way we can work together to fight this epidemic that is trying to rob us of so much more than just our curiosity.

Curiosity helps us to thrive. It is associated with higher levels of positive emotions and lower levels of anxiety.

Curiosity may have killed the cat, but research has shown that with people, curiosity helps us to thrive. It is associated with higher levels of positive emotions and lower levels of anxiety. Remaining curious about things that will help a person grow will also keep a person from falling down into the dark hole of addiction, where the further they fall, the fainter their light becomes.

Curious people who want to learn, who remain coachable, and who are reaching to discover new passions in life get more satisfaction out of life, and they are less likely to reach for a negative vice (like drugs or alcohol) for satisfaction.

Curiosity leads to more participation in school and higher academic achievement and learning because when we are interested in what we are doing, it is easier to get involved and do well and make connections. Curiosity also enhances our empathy. When we are eager to talk with people outside of our social circles, we gain a better understanding of other people's lives and look at the world through a different lens. This also helps in our personal relationships. By asking questions about one another, it demonstrates that you genuinely care for, and respect the other enough to show interest in what is going on with them. Great ideas stem from curiosity and lead to innovation and progress.

Curious people who want to learn, who remain coachable, and who are reaching to discover new passions in life get more satisfaction out of life, and they are less likely to reach for a negative vice (like drugs or alcohol) for satisfaction.

Participation, empathy, asking questions, innovation, and forward movement in life are just some of the side effects of curiosity. Although my curiosity may have been on pause during certain parts of my life, I am happy to say, it is in full effect now.

That is another superpower of remaining curious: you can choose to be curious whenever and wherever you want.

Participation, empathy, asking questions, innovation, and forward movement in life are just some of the side effects of curiosity.

Today, I chose curiosity and a growth mindset over stunting my growth with anything that would prevent me from wanting to learn more about the people, places, and things in this beautiful world I am a small part of.

Today I do not underestimate myself, nor do I place harsh judgment on myself, and I continue to ask questions, to remain coachable. So far, it seems to be working for me.

I challenge you to do as Ted Lasso would do. Be curious, ask the questions, avoid harsh judgment, especially of yourself, and above all…

NEVER UNDERESTIMATE YOUR ABILITY TO KEEP GROWING!

CORE-RELATIONS

(Questions to ask yourself)

🖎 Has there been a time in your life when you felt like you stopped being curious?

_____

_____

_____

🖎 Do you feel like you judge people or things before you have the opportunity to learn more about them?

_____

_____

_____

🖎 In the space provided, write down one thing you are curious to learn more about, along with your plan of action to learn it. Keep it simple and specific. For example: **I am curious about,** "Learning how to sketch pictures of scenery." **Plan of action,** "I will find one YouTuber to watch and learn from and spend thirty minutes a day practicing alongside the video tutorials."

_____

_____

_____

COREAGEOUS Challenge: I encourage you to find time each day dedicated to learning more about the item that strikes your curiosity. The answer to your above question included naming one specific way you will take action. This specific action is your daily goal over the next three weeks. Make it simple and attainable. The goal of this is to become disciplined about this one item so that soon enough, you will learn something new that you've always been curious about!

Share your progress on social media to help you stay accountable, using the hashtags: **#COREageous** and **#COREstrong.** If you are more of a private person and prefer not to share online, write down your daily completion of this **COREAGEOUS Challenge** to help keep yourself on track and accountable.

CHAPTER NINE

PIVOT

When We Cling to What We Know, We Miss the Chance to Grow

BEFORE TED LASSO, there was another chart-topping show called "Friends." If you're sensing a trend of life lessons through movies and television series, you're not wrong. Movies, television, and music are just three examples of entertainment that help me to quiet my mind by getting lost in something else.

Whenever I hear the word, "Pivot," my mind immediately goes back to the iconic episode where Ross, Rachel, and Chandler try to move an oversized couch up the stairs to Ross's new apartment. It was an impossible task to try and maneuver the huge piece of furniture around the tight corners and up the stairwell, which prompted Ross to yell in his ever so dorky, but endearing, voice, **"PIVOT! PIVOT! PIVOT!"** Over and over until Chandler finally loses his cool and screams back at him, **"SHUT UP! SHUT UP! SHUT UP!"**

True story, I had my own couch moment, and many moments in life, where my mind has yelled, *PIVOT! PIVOT! PIVOT!*

It was the mid-nineties, and my husband Brian and I had just moved into our first apartment together. Brian had lived in this apartment for a few years, previous to me moving in.

The apartment building used to be an old factory, which was made into an apartment complex called Gaslight Place. A trendy name with an equally trendy style. Our little apartment seemed much larger than it was, with vaulted ceilings, beautiful exposed wooden beams, exposed pipes, and distressed brick walls. The architecture was something that, at that time, you'd expect to see in a city and not in a quaint New England town, but we loved it. Before long, I gradually started to spruce Brian's bachelor pad into more of a home for us.

Starting, with the couch, otherwise known as "The Bachelor Couch." Now, I won't go into the details of what this bachelor couch looked like, or what may have taken place on said couch, prior to our relationship, but I trust that you can use your own imagination to understand why it had to go. I will just say this, his bachelor couch was slightly nicer than what you might find in a fraternity house.

It was decided. The couch had to go if I was going to stay.

Some people who know me well will say that I am a very determined woman. When I set my mind on doing something, I do it—often without much hesitation. Sometimes this is a very good trait—like when I might be responding to an emergency situation. Other times my go-for-it mindset bites me in the ass—like the day I decided to move The Bachelor Couch out of our apartment and down to the parking garage, where the building dumpsters were located, all by myself.

I had the day off of work and the place to myself, so I decided to use my day off to do a deep cleaning and move some of the furniture around. This was also my opportunity to get rid of The Bachelor Couch and make room for a cleaner and brighter one. Now, I could have probably waited for Brian to get off of work to help me move it—this would have been the logical choice—but I wanted to surprise him. Like I said, when I set my mind on doing something, it gets done, or at least I try to get it done. "Try" being the operative word in this situation.

First, I removed all of the stain-soaked cushions from The Bachelor Couch and put them aside. Next, I began to slide and wiggle the awkward frame inch by inch, through our apartment. It was The Bachelor Couch versus my will. I struggled, pulling, and pushing the beast. Barely out of our front door, I pivoted it to the right and continued the battle down the long and narrow hallway, to the elevator. I wasn't foolish enough to try to use the stairs like Ross, Rachel, and Chandler when I had an elevator at my disposal! *Brilliant*, I thought, *Surely it will fit!*

It did not fit, and I was about to be bitten in the ass.

I shoved The Bachelor Couch into the elevator and began trying to stand it upright, thinking this was yet another logical choice and the best way to go. Pushing, shoving, stomping! Using my back, my legs, anything to get this blast from Brian's past, into the elevator and out of my sight!

Finally, it's in!

Together, the couch and I took the one-floor trip down to the parking garage, saying our final goodbyes.

Ha, I thought to myself, *I won!*

I did not win.

When the elevator door opened, I began to try and wiggle and pivot The Bachelor Couch out, using the same determination I mustered while shoving it into the elevator in the first place.

However, it wouldn't budge. It wouldn't even move a fricking inch. The Bachelor Couch would not leave. It was as if it knew its fate and refused to meet it!

Refusing to give up, I continued with all of my might and willpower, but it was to no avail. The Bachelor Couch was there to stay, or at least until Brian got home from work.

I had no choice but to leave it there, in the elevator, with a note attached to the front of it:

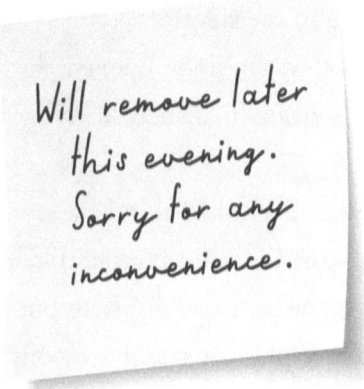

Imagine calling for the elevator, and when it arrives, an old bachelor couch is standing upright on its side, waiting to greet you. Well, for one full day, that is exactly what the other tenants in our building were greeted with each time they called for the elevator. Needless to say, many unhappy people got their steps in that day.

When Brian arrived home after a double shift working as a chef at a local Bistro, he found me sitting in the middle of our living room, watching TV, relaxing on top of a bunch of oversized pillows in place of where The Bachelor Couch once was.

"Valerie." Brian paused, before asking, with a very confused and curious look on his face, "Where's the couch?"

"Ummmm, it's probably better if I show you," I answered, as I got myself up off of the pillows so I could properly greet him with a lengthy kiss and hug in the hopes of buttering him up before walking him down the hallway to show him what was waiting in the elevator.

When the elevator door opened, he just looked at me, shaking his head in disbelief, "Now what the heck did you do?"

That evening, Brian had to take a saw to his bachelor couch to break apart its frame in order to remove it from the elevator, piece by piece. I couldn't help but wonder if there was any type of metaphorical reason why this was happening. Probably not, that's just the artist's brain in me. It likely just boiled down to one determined lady, and one very patient man, starting their lives out together, and the compromises they would have to make along the way. Letting go of what they know, to allow for a chance to grow, together.

Our compromise on that day: The Bachelor Couch finally went, and I stayed.

Compromises, adjustments, responses, pivoting—it is all part of life. Each of us will experience situations where we will have to make our own decision to pivot or remain stuck. When

The Bachelor Couch adapted to its space in the elevator, it remained stuck, that is until Brian's hacksaw came for it.

Pivoting allows us to move fluidly through areas in our life, which would otherwise keep us frozen or stuck and unable to move forward. If we do not have the ability to adjust our responses, our plans, our decisions, and even our emotions, we will settle into spaces, places, and situations that are not good for us. When We Cling to What We Know, We Miss the Chance to Grow.

Pivoting allows us to move fluidly through areas in our life, which would otherwise keep us frozen or stuck and unable to move forward.

Pivoting is an important life skill for many reasons and is essential for maintaining a healthy mind, body, and **CORE**.

I won't rehash how the COVID-19 pandemic sent us all into a pivot, some better than others, but rather I will focus on the three life lessons I have learned from my ability to do so.

When We Cling to What We Know, We Miss the Chance to Grow.

PIVOTING LIFE LESSON №1
When you fall down, get back up!

Seems logical, right? However, some peeps are more naturally resilient than others. Resilience allows a person to thrive in the face of adversity. It allows someone to manage their stress and regain composure without becoming overwhelmed. Inner resilience is a superpower, and a person's ability to tap into it allows them to emerge from pain, struggle, and disappointment, often stronger than before.

In the spring of 2022, my son Collin qualified for the New Balance Nationals Outdoor for the 2k Steeplechase.

The Steeplechase is an event in athletics (in this case, track and field) that derives its name from the steeplechase in horse racing (represented by the runners). In track and field, runners sprint around a four-hundred-meter track, which includes obstacles like water ditches and barriers.

When it came time for Collin to run, I was camped out in the bleachers, near the finish line. Other family members, including my husband, sister, and brother-in-law, were all scattered around the track in order to cheer for him in different areas, all sporting our customized t-shirts my sister had made for her nephew.

"On your marks, get set…GO!" The official commanded, just before pulling the trigger to the starting gun.

They were off. I watched with nervous excitement as Collin made his way around the first half of the track, toward his first attempt over a large barrier into a water ditch. Up and over the barrier he went, propelling strongly toward the end of the water ditch, when suddenly…

HE FELL!

The runner behind him had lost his balance and used Collin to steady himself. While it wasn't intentional, it still sucked for Collin, who was aiming to place high among his field.

It was also incredibly hard to watch. I was heartbroken for him. I was standing next to my friend Michelle, and when Collin fell, she instantly grabbed my arm to reassure me, "He's okay, he's okay." Michelle, being a mother herself, who was also at the race to watch her own son run, understood exactly how I was feeling. Together, we watched Collin immediately get right back up and sprint with all his might to get himself back among the pack of steeplers. Collectively, she and I both sighed with relief.

Although Collin may not have hit his goal for the placement he wanted at Nationals, that was the day we all knew this kid had the ability to literally get back up after a fall and tap into his inner resilience. A gift that is bigger than any medal or placement in the record books, in my opinion.

I also learned what a sense of humor my son has when he shared the video of his fall on Instagram. Collin does not post much on social media, but when he does, it's a pretty damn good share.

Collin's caption under his shared video of his Steeple-chase National Race:

Forgot I wasn't in competitive diving for a minute. Upsetting end to the season at Nats, but I still have two more years to do big things.

Oh, son, the **BEST** is yet to come, and because you have the superpower of resilience, you will certainly do big things; running is just one of them.

Collin's example of resilience was a stumble, a bump in the road, but there are certainly times in life when it is harder to pick ourselves up. There are devastating life events where people will not remain unchanged, and the thought of getting back up after such devastation seems impossible. However, people may also pivot in response to traumatic events and create new paths for themselves. Paths that they never dreamed of, like the one I unearthed for myself after losing my mother to suicide. I never would have dreamed of becoming a published author and inspirational public speaker, but that is what happened when I made the decision to put in the work and turn my pain into purpose. I had the willingness to seek help and to do what was needed to eventually forge through unimaginable pain.

Resilience also comes in the quiet, everyday brave decisions people make.

Resilience also comes in the quiet, everyday brave decisions people make. Resilience after devastating life events does not mean you have to write a book or share your pain with anyone else other than a trusted loved one or a mental health professional. It may look like making the decision to get out of bed, take a shower, and get dressed for the day. It may look like a phone call to a friend to meet up for a walk and just talk for a while. A person's ability to do their best to maintain routines and relationships after devastation IS resilience. It is **COREAGEOUS**, in my book.

While some are born with this superpower or may have it then lose it after trauma, the ability to remain flexible in our thoughts, feelings, and behaviors in response to life events may also be trained.

This is wonderful news for those who are struggling with holding on to hope that things will get better in time. I have learned that time only works if I **DO THE WORK.** Resilience

I have learned that time only works if I DO THE WORK.

is a skill that can be built through partnering with a qualified therapist who focuses on practices to help build this skill. A good therapist to help you to work on your resilience will focus on shifting your mindset, problem-solving, goal setting, effective communication, emotional regulation, stress man-agement, and practicing self-care, aka, **CORE-restoration**, to name a few, but not all at once. A good therapist will build your skill set with one small step at a time until you are walking confidently on your own. The mind is constantly sending signals to the body on how to respond to life events. It is so hopeful to know we can train our minds how to respond, and we have the neuroscience to back this statement up.

PIVOTING LIFE LESSON №2
Just keep swimming

When I was a trainer, I used to hate the terminology, "training to failure." In my profession, it meant repeating an exercise (such as bench press) to the point of momentary muscular failure, or until you simply cannot perform another repetition. I did not like it for a couple of reasons. The word failure has such a negative connotation attached to it, and also it is controversial in the fitness industry whether or not you need to exercise to the point of not being able to perform another rep safely, in order to increase fitness gains. The risk of injury may outweigh the gains.

With any goal in life that you set for yourself, you need to put in the work. Name a goal, any type, personal or professional. What comes naturally for me to share are stories of times when I worked toward a fitness goal.

Shortly after my mother passed away, I trained for my very first sprint triathlon. A sprint triathlon consists of three events. It usually includes a half-mile swim, a twelve-and-a-half-mile bike ride, and a three-mile run, in that order.

At the time of my training, my most comfortable event was the run, and I was also a fairly avid cyclist, but the swimming, well that would be a new sport for me, and one that I decided I needed to hire a coach for.

My gym had a triathlon training program each spring. This program was led by a man named Chris Papsin or

"Papsin," as we all frequently called him. Coach Papsin was not only a colleague but also a personal friend. He came with a lot of experience, as a two-time New England Swimming Champion and also as the head coach of a swim team at a local high school near me. Surely if he could coach high school girls, he could handle me.

My swimming experience was limited, at best. It consisted of years of growing up across the street from my friend Seth, who had a pool where we would play games, like Marco Polo, or jog in one direction, working together to create a massive whirlpool. When we were successful and really got the water going, we would quickly pivot our direction and try to escape the powerful water vortex we created together, imagining that if we didn't, we would somehow all be sucked into its powerful trap, never to emerge from the above ground swimming pool again! They would tell accounts of our disappearance, proving that the tales of the dangers of the swimming pool whirlpools were true after all!

Other than pools, as far as open water swimming, my only other exposure was hanging out at Green Lakes State Park. Green Lakes, located just outside of Syracuse, New York, was the place to be during summer vacation. It was the place to hang-out, not the place to practice your open-water swimming skills, at least not for this girl. No, my time at the lake usually consisted of finding the perfect spot in the sand. An area with enough room to adjust my beach towel in the direction of the ever-changing sun and flip over every so often, reapplying baby oil, to ensure an even tan. The only time I remember going into the lake for any significant goal, other than to quickly cool off, was if the lifeguards blew their whistles, and announced for a human chain to be created to walk inside of the swimming area in order to use our feet to feel for a missing child! Thankfully, the missing child was usually found at the snack bar.

Training to swim in a triathlon would require both pool and open water coaching sessions with coach Papsin, and the rest of the triathletes who were also working on their individual training goals for the same sprint triathlon I had signed up for.

One day during an early morning pool session, Coach Papsin had us practicing what he called, "The Smelly Armpit Drill," better known as a freestyle rotation swimming drill. In this technique, the swimmer, or in my case, the wanna-be swimmer, fully extends their arm on one side, while looking straight down toward the bottom of the pool. Your hips are meant to follow this motion, to avoid lying flat in the water and remain on your side. The swimmer works to keep a strong kick going for approximately eight counts and then takes a stroke to fully extend the opposite arm, while simultaneously keeping their head down and nose in the armpit with a solid rotation through their hips and core. The goal is to help balance out a swimmer's stroke and aide in recovery for the shoulders which are often overtaxed. Ideally, if done properly, this drill works to help put the swimmer into a more streamlined position, getting the full reach and catch of the stroke.

However, for me, the only position this drill was putting me into was a physically and emotionally vulnerable one.

When it came time for me to practice my "Smelly Armpit Drill," I repeated the same things I had been doing each time I tried to swim from one side of the pool to the other. I took a deep breath in and did whatever version of the freestyle swim I could (not sure if there is a name for it) until I needed to come up and gasp for air. When I did pop my head up, I heard coach yell, "Smell your armpit! Smell your armpit! Valerie, take a breath!"

I tried over and over and over and just wasn't getting it. Finally, frustration won. I swam to the edge of the pool, where Papsin was bent down, waiting to talk with me.

"What's going on, how are you feeling?" He asked me, with patience and concern. Now you have to know two things first to fully understand this story.

Number one, Papsin and I frequently busted each other's ass. We both spoke the language of sarcasm very well and could take it as well as dish it out.

Number two, this particular training session was only one week after losing my mom. I was in no mood for the "Stinky Armpit Drill" or sarcasm.

Chris is not only a good peep, but an excellent coach. He sensed that I was not in a good place emotionally to receive his sarcasm or any more cues to smell my armpit. Or maybe he just realized that the water on my face was not only from the pool but also from my tears, as that is what I was reduced to in that moment.

Papsin pivoted from his coaching goals and style for me that day, and it made all of the difference in the overall outcome.

I may have "failed" at that one drill, but the overall goal of completing my first sprint triathlon was a success, even if I did most of the half-mile open water swim, performing the backstroke.

Because of Coach Papsins' ability to pivot, and inspire me to do the same, I literally just kept swimming.

On the day of my triathlon, when it came time for my heat to enter the water, a photographer captured a photo of a sea of swimmers, standing together. All of the swimmers were sporting our pink swim caps, facing in the same direction, looking out onto the water we were about to race into. Well, all except for one, me. I was facing in the exact opposite direction, with my eyes closed, and my hands in prayer position, silently praying to myself, *Lord, please just let me get through this and not drown!*

> *The only way out of most things in life is through them.*

Training for my first triathlon was a reminder that the only way out of most things in life is through them. Although I was one of the last people to emerge from the water in my heat, I did it. I pivoted and got through it to complete my very first sprint triathlon.

I will forever be grateful for Chris's friendship and support to be a better version of myself. Thanks, Pappy, I will remember to always keep swimming in my own unique way.

PIVOTING LIFE LESSON №3
When we cling to what we know, we miss the chance to grow

Have you ever felt unworthy of success? Like maybe you are so used to turmoil and things going wrong that it ruins any chance you have of truly enjoying when things are going well for you? This is what mental health professionals call imposter syndrome. A feeling of being anxious and not worthy of success. Thoughts that despite all of your hard work and good intentions, you are somehow not deserving of the success or good fortune you are receiving.

At times, I have felt like an imposter. As a child of chaos, that was my comfort zone for many years—feelings of not being worthy, like something bad was about to happen because the good times never lasted (or so that was my perception). I walked through most of my life on guard, relating to how Charlie Brown must have felt each time he attempted to kick the football and Lucy swiped the ball out from underneath him. For a good portion of my life, I felt a struggle between trust and betrayal.

Unpacking the details of why I felt so uneasy for decades is not the focus of this book, and some of those details can be found in my first memoir, **SHATTERED TO THE CORE.** In keeping with the goal of this book, I will share the most pivotal decision I made—it brought me to where I am today.

September 17, 2017, I made the decision that I could no longer drink safely. I made the decision that everything I had tried before, and my default coping mechanisms to help me deal with situational bouts of depression and the constant feeling of angst, were not enough, and some of it (like my binge drinking) was harming me. I had to let go of what I knew, or my growth would continue to be stunted.

I could no longer exercise my way out, meditate my way out, clean eat my way out, talk my way out, or drink my way out of feeling stuck or feeling like an imposter. The only way through to the other side was with the help of my community in sobriety. The growth of my mindset, and the emotional and spiritual intelligence I have gained from no longer clinging to my default practices, has given me a healthier perspective about my life, and about life in general.

In literature I have read regarding addiction, they share that you stunt the growth of your mindset, emotional intelligence, and spirituality, the moment you abuse a substance. For me, I chose alcohol, and although I did not drink often, when I did, I never stopped at just one. The goal was always to escape or become something more. More fun, more social, more intelligent, and more comfortable. The irony was, toward the end of my drinking, the more I drank, the more uncomfortable I became in the days and weeks that followed a night of partying.

Often, I share that my sobriety is not my own, and it isn't. True Warriors I have met along the way, have also shared their stories, their lessons, and their hearts, to help me grow and receive the mindset, emotional intelligence, and strong spirit that I have today.

Lessons I have learned from my sobriety include knowing that I no longer have to dwell on my past or be ashamed of it. Now I focus on the moment I am in, and how I have grown from my history. Difficult conversations are no longer something that I avoid. In fact, out of love and respect for others, I know that this is an important thing to do in life in order to understand one another and build strong relationships. Along with difficult conversa- tions, I also do not shy away from conflict resolution, as I have seen the proof of progress in the ability to work through differences. I no longer take things person- ally, and I do my best to remain objective, knowing that people's decisions or the way they may treat me is not about

If you can deeply and maturely understand your emotions, you will not be led by them.

me and none of my business. If you can deeply and maturely understand your emotions, you will not be led by them.

The biggest lesson I have learned from choosing to pivot away from what I knew has been to accept life on life's terms. To live at ease within my **CORE**, knowing that if life decides to pull the football away from me before I have the chance to kick it, I will have a strong foundation in my sobriety, and within my faith, to fall back on.

CORE-RELATIONS

(Questions to ask yourself)

🖋 Has there been a time in your life when you have had to pivot or adjust?

_____

_____

_____

🖋 Have you ever felt like an imposter, unworthy of your successes or achievements?

_____

_____

_____

🖋 In the space provided, list three things you have learned from having to pivot in your life.

_____

_____

_____

COREAGEOUS Challenge: I encourage you to dive deep into this **COREAGEOUS Challenge** and think about a person, place, or thing that you have been afraid to walk toward or away from, that is keeping you from living a more heart-centered life. For example, for me, it was clinging to using alcohol as an unhealthy coping mechanism. The outcome I wanted for myself was peace.

I had to let go of drinking and move toward sobriety. The one thing I picked up to help me toward a more heart-centered life was a recovery program.

Be specific. Name the outcome you want for yourself, and name how you're going to get it. Just writing it down is brave. Now go take the small, everyday steps toward that outcome!

Share your progress on social media to help you stay accountable, using the hashtags: **#COREageous, #COREstrong,** and **#heartcenteredlife.** If you are more of a private person and prefer not to share online, write down your completion of this **COREAGEOUS Challenge** to help keep yourself on track and accountable.

CHAPTER TEN

ZENEMIES

The Peeps Who Zap Your Zen
Are Not Your Friends

IT IS SAID that one of the only birds that dares to peck an eagle is the crow. He sits on the Eagle's back and bites at its neck. The Eagle chooses to not waste his time or energy by responding to the crow. The magnificent Eagle simply opens its wings and begins to rise higher in the sky. The higher the Eagle rises, the harder it is for the crow to breathe and then the crow falls off of the Eagle's back due to lack of oxygen.

I read this analogy during a time in my life when I happened to be shedding some friends who simply tried to zap my Zen, weighing me down from any chance I would have to soar. I wouldn't go so far as to call them my enemy, but rather, a Zenemy.

(According to me), a Zenemy is a peep who is trying to rob me of my Zen. It is a person who disrupts my inner calm, and whose energy disconnects me from my intuition, from the **CORE** of who I am and who I am becoming. Most of us have the innate ability to feel when someone is just not the right person for us to align ourselves with. Our gut tells us when this is happening; all we have to do is trust and listen to our intuition.

I'd like to believe that I really don't have any true enemies out there in the world, but I have absolutely experienced my fair share of Zenemies—we all have—it is one of those unfortunate parts of life.

I have broken these peeps down into three different types of Zenemies:

> ❧ The Zenemy Who No Longer Fits into Your World.
>
> ❧ The Zenemy Who Is Not in Your Corner.
>
> ❧ The Fair Weather Zenemy.

The Zenemy Who No Longer Fits into Your World

Most recently, I have experienced this type of Zenemy in my sobriety from alcohol. My good friends, even the ones who could safely drink, have cheered me on and supported me in my decision not to drink. My Zenemies constantly questioned, and at times, tried to challenge, my decision by saying things like, "I never really noticed you drank all that much. Are you sure you can't have just one drink here or there?" Or another favorite, "I miss buzzed Valerie; she was so much fun!"

Bad friends are **NOT** bad people, just peeps who are no longer the right fit for where you are in your life. Thing is, the ones who do not fit into my sober lifestyle may not have even realized their words and actions were getting in the way of my goals to remain sober, and that is okay. I hold zero resentment or judgment. It is not my responsibility to try to change them either. It is their right to live their life the way that is meant for them, just as much as it is my right to live my life in a way that is meant for me. It also doesn't mean that their way of living is wrong, it only means that it is wrong for me. Therefore, I had to choose to spend less time with the folks who, unbeknownst to them, may have been disrupting the Zen that I have found in sobriety.

This type of Zenemy is a bit more common. You may have experienced it, too, and breaking off this type of friendship can be heartbreaking. This breakup is usually a result of choices made to live your life in a way that differs from someone you once spent a lot of time with. Breaking up is so hard to do, but doing so in a respectful and loving manner can help. There are ways to start putting up boundaries without burning down bridges. Just because someone is not the right person for the season you are in within your life, doesn't mean you have to create a storm. As I stated before when talking about setting boundaries, it is out of respect that we do this. Respect for what you need, as well as respect for what is best for their life. Remember, it is not loving or kind to hold on to people, places, or things that are no longer meant for us.

> *Just because someone is not the right person for the season you are in within your life, doesn't mean you have to create a storm.*

The Zenemy Who Is Not in Your Corner

Another area where I have found Zenemies lurking is when you have a goal or accomplishment to share. In this situation, Zenemies are the ones who have straight-up made fun of or belittled my pursuits. These toxic little Zen stealers are sometimes even bold enough to share their lack of support right to my face, while others choose to take the more cowardly approach and do so behind my back. I have zero time or patience for these types of Zenemies, making them a lot easier to shed. They are often found in your outer social circle. They are the ones trying their best to make you doubt yourself or feel like your goals are unrealistic. These Zenemies that I have come across, have said things to me like, "Are you sure you want to write a book and put all of **THAT** out there?" "How does your family feel about what you are writing?" "What are you trying to prove?"

There is a difference between a friend who offers constructive criticism, looking out for your best interest by offering honesty and encouragement, and a Zenemy who is trying to shut down your goals and dreams completely. A friend operates from a place of love and support, while a Zenemy operates from a place of fear and jealousy. In most cases, you are probably going after something for yourself that they may have also dreamed about, but instead, they let their fears get in the way of their dreams. This led to them feeling jealous, a perfectly normal human emotion. However, it is when they allow that jealousy to get in the way of their support for you that it becomes an issue. When this happens, it is time to shed that Zenemy from your life.

> *A friend operates from a place of love and support, while a Zenemy operates from a place of fear and jealousy.*

The Fair Weather Zenemy

My peeps, my beautiful friendships do not form a circle, nor would I want them to. A circle is closed off, not allowing anyone else to step in. I prefer to remain open and save space for opportunities for the possibility of new friendships to form. One of the things I gained from living a life differently from the way my mother did, is my ability to be vulnerable and to be open. Those who know me also know that I will not hide my pain. I do not view hiding your pain as a **COREAGEOUS** attempt at life. It is unfair to laugh with our friends but cry alone. Great friendships share both laughter and heartache. Sharing your pain can also be a good way to filter out the fair-weather Zenemies.

It is unfair to laugh with our friends but cry alone.

While many of the peeps in your life may be down for a good time, the ones who rise to the top are the ones who will step up and be there for you when things are not going so well. They're there for the painful times; they will be there without question or hesitation. These people may not even be someone you know all that well, which is why my friendships do not form a circle, leaving room for others to come into my life, leading to an unexpected new relationship. This is God's work, placing angels in your life for reasons that cannot be explained.

These angels also make up for the disappointment and loss you may feel in the harsh realization that the ones you held close in your life were not capable of rising to the challenge when you needed them most. The ones who lacked the capacity to be there during your challenging seasons are the fair-weather Zenemies. The fair-weather Zenemies are not necessarily people you should cut out of your life, but rather, just be aware of what their emotional capacity is. They are the fun ones, the acquaintances in your life. Not bad people, just there for the surface stuff, offering a fun time, lots of laughter, and small talk. You may have thought of them as close friends, but when you were seeking shelter from their friendship during a storm, they took their umbrella and ran. In the long run, you are better off not directing your energy toward nurturing this type of friendship. This discovery is a gift. It allows for the right peeps to enter into your life.

I have experienced all three types of these Zenemies throughout my life.

> **"I wanna see you eat, just not at my table."**
>
> Tupac Shakur

Just because I may have lost some of the peeps in the above categories as my friends, I certainly hope I have never gained any actual enemies in the process. I wish the same things for these people (whose friendships I have chosen to no longer nurture) and for their loved ones as I wish for myself and my loved ones.

I am a woman of spiritual faith and connection to God, a God who calls us to love our Zenemies as much as we love ourselves. This is to say, we want to see them be the best variation of their true self, living their best life, but no longer a part of ours. One of the many key things I learned in my recovery group came from my first sponsor. I was struggling with a certain relationship in my life, and she suggested

I pray for that person. She told me to specifically pray for the same things I would want for anyone I loved and to do this for three straight weeks. She said we would revisit this subject to see how I felt after praying with these intentions.

After three weeks, what I discovered was the "peace that surpasses all understanding," one of my favorite Bible passages. It works if ya work it, as I have learned from those who have shared their experiences, strength, and hope with me.

Friendships are a beautiful and important part of life. They have a major impact on our mental health and well-being. I am a strong believer in maintaining connections as one of the most important tools for remaining in good mental health. Believe me, I am all for my alone time. However, there is a difference between *being* alone and *feeling* alone.

There is a difference between being alone and feeling alone.

Isolation and loneliness is a dangerous rabbit hole to fall down, and one that I believe ultimately led to my mother's death.

Healthy friendships that celebrate your good times and support you during your bad times are a true gift. While wrapping up the final edits of this book, I turned fifty years old. A few months prior to this milestone birthday, my sister Monica asked me what I would like to do. I expressed to her that if I could have anything in the world for my birthday, it would be to spend it surrounded by the closest women in my life, making more meaningful connections. A spa came to mind, but I realized this would be an incredibly extravagant gift and request. Well, Monica did what she does best and planned the most amazing weekend at a spa, where some of my closest girlfriends showed up to help celebrate by joining in a very special surprise birthday dinner.

I knew about the spa weekend, and that I would be spending it with Monica as well as my lifelong and dear friend, Kimberly.

The moment I arrived at the spa they both made me feel so special. I gave the front desk my name, and the receptionist said, "Welcome, Valerie. I hear you are the lady of the hour. Happy Birthday to you! I have some special items for you." She handed me a mocktail, along with a fiftieth birthday crown and matching sash to wear, and directed me to my room. There, I found both Monica and Kimberly anxiously waiting for me to walk into our room with music blasting from the Beatles, "THEY SAY IT'S YOUR BIRTHDAY!" And a life-sized 5-0 adorned with gold and black balloons, handmade by Kimberly, who also cautiously traveled with them from Syracuse. Monica also traveled from Syracuse, with many surprises and a full, but relaxing, itinerary that, unbeknownst to me, included a surprise birthday dinner on our final night at the spa.

I had no idea, no inclination at all, and this plan apparently had been six months in the making. When we walked downstairs to have dinner together on our final night, I thought it would just be the three of us, and followed the host to a private room, where a roomful of most of the closest ladies in my life were waiting for me.

I cried. For numerous reasons, I cried; being surprised was just one of them.

I cried because of the importance each of these women has in my life. My friends, my sister, my daughter—all of them together in one room overwhelmed me. What was once a self-declared battle for so many years—trying to fit in and be accepted by people who would honestly love and support me—was now available for me to recognize, honor, and enjoy. I cried because I understood the maneuvering each one of the ladies in that room had to do in order to be there. But mostly, I cried because of the awareness of how lucky I was, and how my sister also knew that the most important thing for me at this time in my life was for my friends and family to know how much I love them because the same is also true for her. Monica and I have experienced the profound loss of time and not having another tomorrow to say what you want to say. We don't wait for another tomorrow to love, to live, and to celebrate. That evening we celebrated with both tears and plenty of laughter. I will never forget it.

Friendships increase our sense of belonging and give us purpose. They improve our self-confidence and self-worth. Friendships with similar values are even more meaningful because they help to promote personal growth and development. Those meaningful connections are a key factor in both our mental and physical health. There have been many studies conducted proving that people who maintain healthy relationships, connections, and fellowships live longer and happier lives than their peers with fewer connections.

> *Friendships with similar values are even more meaningful because they help to promote personal growth and development.*

This is one of the most important items I talk about when advocating the preventative measures we can take to stay in good mental health.

Here are a few ways you may make new friends or nurture existing friendships:

- Join a local gym and take group fitness classes
- Introduce yourself to neighbors—do a rotating dinner party or card game
- Volunteer with a local non-profit
- Attend your local community events
- Extend and accept invitations
- Take up a new interest or hobby
- Join a faith community
- Reconnect with old friends

Above all, remember it is never too late to do as my favorite Girl Scout song says, only this time with updated life lesson lyrics:

> Make new friends, as the Zenemies
> unfold, one is silver and
> the other gold.

We can all take lessons from the eagle that chooses not to fight the crow even though it is biting him. When we choose to rise, rather than exhausting our energy toward our Zenemies' bites at our CORE, soon enough they will fall away as we ascend.

Do not allow yourself to succumb to the distractions caused by Zenemies; keep your focus on doing the next right thing and keep rising above.

CORE-RELATIONS

(Questions to ask yourself)

❧ In your life, have you experienced any of the three types of Zenemies? If so, which one(s)? The Zenemy who no longer fits into your world, the one not in your corner, or the fair weather Zenemy?

_____

_____

_____

❧ Based on your answer to the question above, write a prayer for your Zenemy.

_____

_____

_____

❧ In the space provided, list three ways you will make new friends or nurture existing friendships.

_____

_____

_____

COREAGEOUS Challenge: I encourage you to choose one of the ways you will make new friends or nurture existing friendships and carve out time at least once a week to do so for yourself. Make it simple and attainable. The goal of this is to become disciplined about this one item, so that soon enough, it becomes a healthy habit, and you will develop new and/or deeper connections.

Share your progress on social media to help you stay accountable, using the hashtags: **#COREageous** and **#COREstrong.** If you are more of a private person and prefer not to share online, write down your weekly completion of this **COREAGEOUS Challenge** to help keep yourself on track and accountable.

CHAPTER ELEVEN

I LIKE BEING AN OUTSIDER

Grace Among This Place

I WAS FOUR years old when I experienced my first serious bout of sun-stroke. Or at least that is what my grandmother called it. I believed her because she was a trained nurse and just about the most capable woman I knew. Plus, I also knew better than to question her; she was one tough lady!

What I remember of that day is playing outside of my grandparents' home, in a little suburban town just outside of Syracuse, New York. My grandparents watched over me while my mother was at work. I was playing with some of the kids in their neighborhood on a hot and muggy afternoon in July. We often played together. We would run across the open backyards, no matter if we knew whose property it was. The entire neighborhood welcomed our play along with our boundless energy. We were not discouraged by fences or made to feel that we were trespassing. It was the 70s, a time when our lives seemed much simpler. A time when the fresh-cut grass smell in the air would call us to take off our shoes, run barefoot through the sprinklers, and slide down homemade water slides from collected Hefty bags. We would play for hours, with music in the background, blaring from boom boxes set up in the windows for everyone to hear. Radios blasted songs from Fleetwood Mac, Led Zepplin, The Who, and Lynyrd Skynyrd, to name a few.

On this particular summer day, I had been playing in the sandbox of a neighbor's yard—at least that was the last thing I remember. The next image that comes to mind, is of an older man, standing over the top of me reassuring me with words like, "You're okay, you're okay," while I lay on the carpet of my grandparents' living room. This man was an EMT who apparently heard the screams from my grandmother for somebody to come help me. He rushed over and started CPR. I was having heatstroke, and my little body was literally on fire with a temperature above 104 degrees. I am not sure how long I stopped breathing, but from the stories, it wasn't long, just long enough to learn that I was very prone to overheating, otherwise known in my family as sun-stroke.

From that day on, rightfully so, my nervous mother would constantly remind me to look out for the warning signs of overheating. Signs like nausea, dizziness, red face, and so on. What I would mostly experience was migraines. Overheating was one of the triggers for the onset of my debilitating migraines. So, I was very careful not to let that happen. I would take timed breaks in the shade to place cool cloths across the back of my neck and drink more water than I probably needed. As I write this, it is making me accept the fact that this experience is probably why I became a mother who is infamous for protecting her own children from getting overheated or sunburnt. Maybe someday they will thank me for their beautiful porcelain skin.

As cautious as that experience made me, I was also very careful not to let heatstroke take over my love of being an "outsider."

Being an outsider—a nature nut, granola girl, gnarly, dirtbag—who treks NOBO and SOBO on any trail that provides the opportunity to learn more outdoorsy slang (NOBO and SOBO—Appalachian Trail slang for Northbound or Southbound thru-hiker) or, more importantly, about herself. That is who I am.

I am lucky enough to live minutes from the first trail town that thru-hikers going Northbound (NOBO) come to when hiking the Appalachian Trail and reaching the state of Connecticut. The Appalachian Trail, also known as the AT, extends across fourteen states. Going Northbound, it begins at Springer Mountain in Georgia and ends at the summit of Mount Katahdin in Maine. It is roughly 2,200 miles. Each year, hundreds of hikers set out to walk the entire trail in a single season. Me, I set out for sections of it whenever I have the chance. Most recently, I have become what is known as a LASHer (Long-Ass-Section-Hiker). Until I am able to take more time off from the demands of my off-trail life, I will continue to strap on my pack and LASH my way through sections of the AT, while balancing my vacation days out on the trail and with family.

I am so grateful to live where I do. But truthfully, when I first moved from New York to Connecticut, it was a huge change, and for a time, I thought it was also a huge mistake.

It was my twenty-first birthday, and I had only been a resident of Connecticut for a few short months. I worked in the deli department of a local family-owned grocery store called Northville Supermarket. I loved my job there and the family I worked for, the Brenners. It was a fun job where I also made some of my first friends after moving to the Nutmeg State.

On the day of my twenty-first birthday, I was scheduled to work a long shift. I had intended to head home after, when my friend Lindel convinced me to go out with her and a bunch of others to a local pub to celebrate. Always up for a good time and adventure, I agreed.

When we arrived at the Marble Dale Pub, there was a band playing and a few locals dancing on the small and sticky dance floor. My friends loved to play pool, so they placed their quarters down on the side of the pool table and claimed the opportunity to take on the winners of the next game.

"Come on Valerie," Lindel and Kevin said to me, "Let's play some darts while we wait for the next game."

This is where I had my first of a few "WTF" moments and stark reality checks. *Where the hell Podunk town did I just move to*, I panicked. It was not at all what I was used to or expected.

You see, a twenty-first birthday in Syracuse would have likely been spent bar hopping downtown, near the SU Campus, where no darts or pool would be involved, but plenty of sticky club dance floors would be. I think the stark contrast of growing up in a fairly suburban area by a large university, to living in a quiet New England town threw me. It would take some getting used to.

After our night was over, I called my friend Kimberly back home in Syracuse, in tears. I described my twenty-first birthday celebration in my new home of the Nutmeg State at the Marble Dale Pub, while she just listened and reassured me that everything would get better with more time to get adjusted.

It was an adjustment, to say the least. One that, in time, I would come to love and friends who I would also love and hold dear in my heart (and still do to this day), even though our lives have brought us to different places. Soon, I came to like playing pool and became one hell of a dart player, hitting a few tops and not just the rail of the board. Before there was hiker slang for me to learn, there was dart player slang for me to master.

One of the ways I came to love my new home was through running. Hitting the pavement and the trail allowed me to get to know my surroundings and discover endless attributes about my new home. It would also prove that I was an outsider, at heart.

Before long, what used to make me feel uneasy and out of place would be the one place I would frequent to become reacquainted with peace. The woods, my church. A place where my worries and stresses could be alleviated in the untamed spaces within the vastness of the opportunities to do so that Mother Nature has freely given us. She asks nothing in return, and gives so much of herself, any time that we ask. If we respect Mother Nature's beauty and her power, she will teach us grace.

If we respect Mother Nature's beauty and her power, she will teach us grace.

That is one of the many gifts that being an outsider has taught me.

Grace.

In my first book, I closed with a quote, **"From Mother Nature's roots, I will grow."** As I write this today, I am still growing and will continue, especially in my ability to show and feel grace. As a self-proclaimed type A former control freak (I say former because I do believe I have improved my ability to let go of things that are none of my business or out of my control, most days), the feeling of relief that grace will give you, once you allow yourself to not only give it to others but also to yourself, is tremendous.

It was Columbus weekend, 2022. Me and my "Early Birdie" girlfriends planned a weekend getaway hike in the White Mountains of New Hampshire. "Early Birdies" was a nickname we gave ourselves when we used to get up at the crack of dawn to meet at our local gym or go for a run together, but post-COVID, our schedules shifted, as did our physical goals. Cheryl, Alice, Audrey, Laura, Cathy, and myself, aka the "Early Birdies."

One thing that we all loved to do, and still could do together, despite our numerous injuries and wear and tear from all of our collective weekend warrior adventures, was to hike. On this particular trip, we planned to hike Mount Lafayette.

Mount Lafayette is a 5,249-foot mountain at the northern end of the Franconia Range in the White Mountains of New Hampshire. You gain about four thousand feet of elevation along the nine strenuous miles of this loop. The weather in the White Mountains is unpredictable and can go from sunny skies at the base, to wind, rain, sleet, and/or snow at the summit. It is important to be prepared, and on the day the ladies and I set out to summit Lafayette. What I would discover was the importance of grace.

On the morning of our adventure, we were all excited. We rented a cozy little home, just south of the mountain where we arrived the evening before in order to be well rested and prepared.

"Who wants coffee?" Alice asked everyone, to which we all replied with a resounding, "ME!" It was early, and we were all tired but also excited to get going. Together, we packed up our day packs with the peanut butter and jelly sandwiches we made the night before, as well as homemade goodies from Audrey, co-owner of a very successful local res-taurant known for their comfort food and baked goods. We knew we could count on her to bring the good stuff! Along with Audrey's sugary treats, we packed plenty of water, trail mix, and dates. Dates, an inside joke among us birdies, are nutritionally dense and provide a healthy energy option; they counterbalanced Miss Muffin's, aka, Audrey's, cookies, which were the size of your face! After braiding Cheryl's hair, with our packs in place, we headed out the door for the trailhead.

It was 7:00 a.m. when we got started and the weather, as expected, was freezing. As we approached the trailhead, the trail-boss volunteers at Lafayette Place asked if we had spikes. "You're gonna need them for the ridge," he warned us. "It gets pretty slick up there this time of year." We nodded, as most of us packed micro spikes in our day packs.

Within the first few steps, I could already feel my right knee. This knee has been a source of pain for me, on and off for the past five years. Torn meniscus and arthritis, both leading to a Baker's Cyst that likes to rear its annoying head from time to time to remind me of my injuries.

On the day of the hike, my Baker's Cyst was progressively getting worse, and I could now feel it between a joint space, restricting my range of motion and ability to push off of my right foot.

Just over one mile in, I took a step and winced in pain, feeling totally unstable in my gait.

"Ladies, this is it for me. I'm going to turn around," I said to the Early Birdies, finally admitting to all of them, and to myself, just how bad my knee was.

They spent the next several minutes trying to talk me out of it before realizing there was no use, and I was decidedly done. With this realization, each one of them offered to turn back with me. That is just the type of crew I roll with, each one more generous than the next. "Let me go with you," Laura said with deep empathy in her eyes, followed by the same sentiments among the others until I genuinely reassured them that I was good in my decision.

"I'm sorry Valerie," Cathy said as she stopped her ascent to turn and check in with me, "But hey, we can always do this again!" reassuring me with her contagious positive perspective.

"Buddy, are you okay?" Cheryl stood just ahead of me. We always call each other buddy, not sure why or how that began, but on the trail at that moment, it was said in the most endearing way. "Buddy, I'm sorry. Are you sure you don't want us to turn back?" she added.

"No, please don't. That would make me feel so much worse, I swear!" I would have felt awful ruining everyone else's weekend because of a decision I had to make for myself.

With that, I turned back, surrendering to the fact that it was just not going to happen today. To continue forward would be making a decision based on ego and placing each of my friends in danger the further I ascended to try to prove something to myself.

Sometimes in life, it is all about timing.

So instead, I descended and began a very painful trek back down toward the base of the mountain where I was greeted by the same trail-boss as when we first set out.

"What happened, where are your friends?" he asked me.

"Oh, just battling an old knee injury. It's not in the cards for me today."

"Don't worry, this mountain ain't going nowhere. It will be here for you when you return." Sometimes in life, it is all about timing.

It was something about not only that trail-boss's wise words but also the way he spoke to me that day, that reminded me of how much I have grown as a person. How much of that growth has been by being an outsider? Truth is, if that situation had happened just a few years prior, turning back would have had me in tears, or worse yet, I may have pushed myself too hard and made my injury even worse. But that morning I chose to surrender and raise my white flag, and I was truly at peace with it. I felt exactly how the trail-boss described it, but I didn't have the words. The mountain would still be there when I returned, and a plan to climb that mountain with my husband, would also be in my future. That's the thing about mountains. They have an undeniable presence that is unwavering and demands respect. That day I needed to grant both Mount Lafayette and me the respect we deserved.

Often our strength does not lay in resistance and our ability to push through pain, but rather, in the ability to muster the strength to show ourselves respect and a little grace.

That experience also reaffirmed that often our strength does not lay in resistance and our ability to push through pain, but rather, in the ability to muster the strength to show ourselves respect and a little grace.

That day turned out to be a good day, despite it not going the way I planned, and grace allowed me to feel that way about it. This mindset came over time as I tried my best to shift away from the default of frustration or avoidance in that moment and failing to honor my injury. This is not to say I didn't feel sad or frustrated, I did. The difference was that I could now feel those very human emotions and make the decision to shift my mindset into a positive, productive, and peaceful place. This habit-forming mindset took time and practice.

Everything that is worthwhile in life happens over slow progress, and not all at once.

Everything that is worthwhile in life happens over slow progress, and not all at once, just like in nature. The beauty we admire about Mother Nature has developed over time; she does not rush. Tiny seeds transform into saplings that eventually become strong oak trees. Lessons take time. Greatness takes time. Grace doesn't just happen, just like the smooth patterns of river stones don't just happen. The path to the state of grace is carved out through time, trial, surrender, and love. This state of being is a gorgeous place to be.

The path to the state of grace is carved out through time, trial, surrender, and love. This state of being is a gorgeous place to be.

Being an outsider is the heart of who I am. But the trail has shown me so much more than which direction to hike—north or southbound—it has shown me the path to grace.

I think I'll continue to trek down this path of grace and being an outsider; it seems to be working for me.

CORE-RELATIONS

(Questions to ask yourself)

🖋 Is there something in your life that you have grown to love over time that perhaps you may not have enjoyed at first, just as I have by moving from more of a city to country life?

_____

_____

_____

🖋 Has there been a time in your life when you had to make a heartbreaking decision not to continue something? If so, what was it and what were your feelings around that decision?

_____

_____

_____

🖋 In the space provided, please write what grace means to you.

_____

_____

_____

COREAGEOUS Challenge: I encourage you to carve out ten minutes each day over the next three weeks to find time to get outside. It doesn't have to be anything grand, just a minimum of ten minutes, or more if that suits you, dedicated to getting some fresh air despite whatever the weather conditions are where you live. Make it simple and attainable. The goal of this is to become disciplined about this one item so that soon enough, it becomes a healthy way of boosting your mood, self-esteem, and overall wellbeing.

Share your progress on social media to help you stay accountable, using the hashtags: **#COREageous, #COREstrong,** and **#CORErestoration.** If you are more of a private person and prefer not to share online, write down your daily completion of this **COREAGEOUS Challenge** to help keep yourself on track and accountable.

CHAPTER TWELVE

IRISH TWINS

The Luck of the Irish

MY SISTER AND I are Irish Twins. This terminology is believed to have originated from the stereotype that Irish families are known to have many children born one after another. I am not sure there is truth in that assumption about the Irish, as my mother only had two children; however, we were only eleven months apart and often we were both referred to as Irish Twins.

Although we are close in age, truth is, we experienced our fair share of growing pains, as most siblings undoubtedly do, beginning with my earliest memory of the painful experience of starting Kindergarten.

I am not sure whose idea it was to have Monica and me begin our elementary school years together, but it wouldn't last long. I would "fail" Kindergarten, which would turn out to be a good thing, giving us a chance to develop our own identities and friendships, one school year apart.

Fall, 1979

It was our first day of Kindergarten. Together, Monica and I walked into the front doors of Minoa Elementary School wearing our matching skirts and cowl neck sweaters. Our legs were covered by tights to keep us warm from the crisp fall air in Central New York.

Our mother had just re-married after years of being a single mom. My horrible step-father insisted on adopting Monica and me and giving us his name—a gesture that was more about power than genuine love. Along with this new "dad" of ours came a new last name for both of us.

"M-o-y-n-i....." I recited over and over, whispering to myself, trying to learn and remember how to spell my foreign and ridiculously long last name. Instinctively, I didn't like it one bit. It didn't fit, and somehow, even at five years old, I knew what my mother would take ten years to realize. But I also knew that my teacher would likely ask me to spell out my last name, and I did not want to draw any attention to the fact that I really did not know or understand why I had to have a new last name in the first place, let alone how to spell it out.

"You'll get it in time; just keep practicing." My mother reassured me, while extending her left hand out for me to grab, as Monica was already holding tightly onto her right hand. Monica didn't say a word the entire time we made our way through the busy lobby that was full of proud parents, happy children, and teachers. They were all bustling about headed to wherever they would start their first day of school.

And then there was us. The three musketeers as we often thought of ourselves. My mom, my sister, and me.

"Good morning Monica and Valerie. Welcome to Minoa Elementary!" The principal warmly greeted us, directing us to our classrooms. I am not sure why, but I remember assuming that Monica and I would naturally be in the same class. We were always together; we were Irish Twins! Surely our elementary school would know to respect this fact and keep our union going, even in a classroom setting.

They did not.

"Come this way, let me show you to your classrooms," the principal said as he walked Monica toward one room. I followed close behind, ready to enter along with her. Instead, he turned to block my entry, "Ah, ah, ah. No, Valerie, your classroom is right next door, over here."

Instantly, I felt my heart drop quickly into my stomach. It felt like the principal just ripped a literal body part off me and then expected me to go about my day as if nothing happened. I was traumatized and decided then and there that I hated Kindergarten already, and the first bell hadn't even rung!

Reluctantly, I walked into my classroom and noticed a door off to the right toward the back corner of the room. It had a window and I decided to see if it could be a possible escape route. It wasn't. However, I did learn that this door separated my classroom from my sister's. It was also a door that, for the next three months, I would stand next to and pathetically peer through the window into the room that held my Irish Twin captive for six whole hours. Six of the longest hours we had ever been apart. This might have been both a bit dramatic and co-dependent, but my sister was my safety blanket, and that school tried to take her from me–at least that is how Five-Year-Old Me felt at that time.

I didn't last long in that Kindergarten class. I believe it was during Christmas break, after crying and begging to see my sister every day for three straight months, that my schoolteacher finally pulled my mother in to discuss holding me back a year. It was evident to all that I was not emotionally ready to start Kindergarten, and it would be in everyone's best interest if we tried again the following year.

That decision turned out to be a very smart one. It allowed Monica and me to develop our own identities, friendships, styles, and opinions. Soon, we would discover we were more unalike than alike. Soon, we would go from tears that we couldn't be together, to tears from the frustration of being together too much.

The elementary days were pretty light and carefree, despite the underlying chaos in our home, and the two of us got along pretty well. Well enough to share a bedroom with adjacent canopy beds that had a similar style and décor—feminine, seventies, and whatever our mother picked out for us. We had the same taste in Saturday morning cartoons and cereal. We held the same affection for all of our animals (our bunnies, birdies, and fishes), and we shared the responsibilities of caring for them.

It wasn't until middle school, or likely when hormones started to invade our little Irish Twin bodies, that we began to fight, and our fights were full of everything: emotions, tears, frustration, rage, anger, jealousy, misunderstanding, confusion, and immaturity. Our fights were epic, and our bond would be tested time and time again, but each time we were tested, somehow love would win. Despite all of the yelling, curling iron throwing, and threatening by my sister to padlock her closet in a valid attempt to keep me from stealing all of her clothes, we would find our way back to the closeness we were naturally born into.

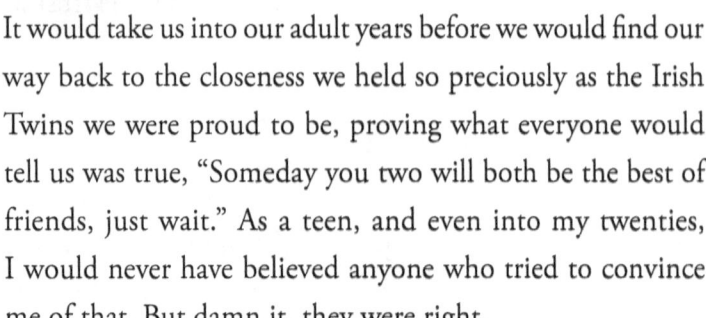

It would take us into our adult years before we would find our way back to the closeness we held so preciously as the Irish Twins we were proud to be, proving what everyone would tell us was true, "Someday you two will both be the best of friends, just wait." As a teen, and even into my twenties, I would never have believed anyone who tried to convince me of that. But damn it, they were right.

Slowly, Monica and I began developing a mutual respect. I can't say exactly when that happened, but I do know that the moment she became a mother, and I met my nephew, everything changed.

Fall, 1997

Monica was pregnant with her first child, my nephew, Bryce.

On his due date, she went to her scheduled checkup with her obstetrician. She had been fighting a really bad headache for a week prior to this appointment. Her doctor checked her blood pressure and discovered it was dangerously high (180/100). With that, her doctor ordered her to go straight to the hospital.

Monica left the appointment, grabbed her husband, Bruce, from work, and followed her doctor's orders.

There, the nurses started Monica on Pitocin, (a synthetic hormone expectant mothers are often given to help induce labor). Except the Pitocin was not working on her body.

By the following morning, more bloodwork was now coming, which revealed alarming information that showed both her kidneys and liver were failing from her condition of pre-eclampsia. Rarely, pre-eclampsia can take a dangerous turn, and unfortunately, my sister's had.

Things moved very quickly from there. The nurses informed Monica and Bruce that they were going to have to do an emergency Cesarean section and deliver the baby. They also told Bruce that he would not be allowed in the operating room (dads are usually allowed in non-emergency Cesarean births) because Monica would be put completely under anesthesia.

Monica had no choice in what happened next, and I can only describe how terrifying and desperate those next moments were for her based on the details she shared with me.

"Am I going to die?" Laying on the gurney, Monica looked up at Bruce, right before they wheeled her into the operating room.

With no chance for her husband to offer words of comfort, Monica was given paperwork and felt as though she was signing her life away.

Next, more nurses and orderlies gathered around her gurney, grabbed the signed paperwork from her trembling hands, and ran her down the hallway, rushing toward the operating room, where she was greeted by another set of doctors and nurses.

"Okay Monica, we will have to secure your arms in a T-position, away from your sides, so we are able to perform the surgery. This is for yours and the baby's safety," one nurse explained.

With that, Monica began to silently start praying to herself, and for her unborn child, over and over again.

"Whatever you are doing Monica, keep doing it. It is working." The anesthesiologist calmly whispered into her ear, after observing on the monitor that her blood pressure was slowly beginning to come down.

"Hail Mary, full of Grace..."

I remember getting the phone call from my mother, updating me on what was happening. Our mom had traveled from Connecticut to Syracuse to be with my sister while she remained in the hospital for one week after delivering a healthy baby boy. I came the following week to help out when she was released to recover at home.

Apparently, by now, the entire family was placing bets to see if I would cry upon meeting my nephew for the first time, with me betting that I would not. At the time of his birth, I really didn't have any instinctual motherly or auntie emotions running through me—that is until I walked through the front door of my sister and brother-in-law's home and laid eyes on him.

There he was, wrapped in a blue blanket, nestled warmly and tightly in my sister's arms. She looked exhausted, but so in love.

"May I hold him?" I asked, cautiously. He was so tiny, so beautiful, so miraculous.

"Of course you can," Monica said, as Bruce took him from her arms and carefully placed him in mine.

I don't think I had ever held a newborn baby before that day, and I know for sure I had never experienced the emotions that followed after my auntie and motherly instincts kicked in.

I lost the bet I placed on myself as tears began to well up in my eyes and fall down my face. I was unable to wipe them away, and I didn't mind either. No, my hands were doing something much more important. They were holding onto my newborn nephew.

From that day on, everything changed for the better between Monica and me. Not to say that we didn't have our fair share of bumps along the way, but that was the day that the importance of family was reaffirmed between Monica's new and growing family and the family I would eventually make for myself just three short years after she had her first child.

We began to prioritize our children spending time together—Bryce, Bailey, and Collin. We began to see one another's differences as strengths and admire them for what they were, instead of criticizing or judging. It is a beautifully **COREAGEOUS** view to have when you can acknowledge one's differences as strengths to admire rather than resorting to criticism.

> *It is a beautifully COREAGEOUS view to have when you can acknowledge one's differences as strengths to admire rather than resorting to criticism.*

We began to respect one another for the mothers we became and supported each other through the difficult times motherhood inevitably brought. When the time came that we had to bury our own mother unexpectedly and tragically, we grew even closer from our own unspeakable and individual pain. Our adult relationship has allowed us to speak to one another in ways we had never had the courage to do before.

> *It is common for people to hold back in relationships when they have been hurt.*

There are now "I love you's being said. There is now an honesty about the hardships of life, shared between us without the judgment that we once held onto, built up by our own personal fears. It is common for people to hold back in relationships when they have been hurt. The opposite was true for Monica and me. Our pain gave us an understanding of how precious and important our time together is, and we make that time count.

So much so, that as I write this chapter, I have just returned from a surprise girls' night out that Monica planned for us. No special occasion—just because we both want to make more wonderful memories and less sad ones now, together.

Fall, 2023

I pulled up to my sister's home in Chittenango, New York, shortly after 2:00 p.m. to find her anxiously awaiting my arrival.

"Are you ready for a fun girls' night?" Monica asked with great enthusiasm, barely able to contain the secret she had been keeping for the last two months.

"I am!" I answered, and with that, we packed up her car and hit the road.

We were five minutes into our drive when my sister began to play a song from her playlist.

Morning, just another day
Happy people pass my way
Looking in their eyes
I see a memory
I never realized
How happy you made me

Oh, Mandy
Well, you came, and you gave without taking
But I sent you away

Oh, Mandy
Well, you kissed me and stopped me from shaking
And I need you today
Oh, Mandy

~ Barry Manilow

"Good God, please tell me we are not listening to Barry Manilow the whole road trip!" I exclaimed, immediately triggered into the nightmare of memories from our youth. Thinking back to the countless amount of times I wanted to stab my own eardrums out to spare them from having to listen to my sister attempt that very song on her Andy Gibb guitar.

"Oh yeah baby," she enthusiastically answered, her face displaying a devilish grin, but I still wasn't picking up on the clues she was dropping. She continued, "We will be listening to him all night long! ALL NIGHT LONG!" She shouted.

Stumped, I just stared blankly at her. Finally, she couldn't hold the surprise in any longer and screamed, "WE'RE GOING TO SEE BARRY MANILOW!!! SEVENTH ROW, BABY! He is playing at the Turning Stone Casino!"

"You're kidding me?!" I respond with both confusion and excitement. Confusion because honestly, I didn't know he was still alive! Excitement, because I could see by my sister's face that she had put a lot of effort and thought into this evening, and this was not lost on me.

"I got us a room in the tower at the casino. Everything is right there, including the restaurant and the concert venue. Then we just head upstairs to our room; it's gonna be awesome!" Monica explained the itinerary and went on to tell me how she planned the whole thing out, once again utilizing her knack for planning and making things very special for others to enjoy.

When we arrived at the Turning Stone Casino, we checked into our rooms and learned we were on the top floor. We took the next hour to freshen up and get ready to head downstairs for dinner.

Monica was dressed in a stunning silk skirt, pink silk blouse, sparkly heels, and a sparkly handbag to match. I was in jeans and a sequined burgundy top, wearing flat black dress shoes and no matching bag, but rather a side sling turquoise fanny pack.

Looking at my shoes and bag, Monica asked with concern, "Seriously, are those the shoes you are wearing and the bag you are bringing?"

> Accepting someone's individuality allows us to break free from the confines of our narrower perspectives and opens up the opportunity to look through a broader lens.

"Yes, why? Are they that bad? I mean, they are both very practical!" We both cracked up at the differences we still have and the newfound appreciation of those differences. Accepting someone's individuality allows us to break free from the confines of our narrower perspectives and opens up the opportunity to look through a broader lens.

Although there is not a one-size-fits-all approach as to how we each live our lives. Monica decided to stick with her style, and so did I.

> There is not a one-size-fits-all approach as to how we each live our lives.

With our individual styles in place, Monica smelling of perfume by Chrisitan Dior and me with an earthy Tea Tree Oil scent, we headed downstairs.

When dinner was over, we decided we would spend twenty dollars each trying our luck at the penny slots before we headed upstairs to the concert. We stuck to that limit, for the most part. Neither of us came out as winners from testing our luck at the slots.

However, that night was a win for us as sisters, and we were lucky in a different way. We were lucky to be one another's Irish Twin.

We spent the next two hours, singing along with the master of cheesy tunes and his cohorts of self-proclaimed "Fanilows."

Before long, Barry, with his silky voice and heartfelt lyrics, began to draw me in. Monica and I couldn't help but sing and dance along to hits like, "I Can't Smile Without You," "I Write the Songs," "Copacabana," and of course, our favorite, "Mandy."

By the time Barry began to sing the song that, at one time, used to make me want to stab myself in the eardrums, I was already transformed into a "Fanilow." My eyes were glued to the stage as a video was played for the audience. It was from an old clip of the first time he performed, live on television, the hit that made him famous. As the clip began to play out, and it was time for the second verse, the stage lights shifted over to shine down on Barry Manilow, who was seated at his piano, adorning the same bedazzled jacket (perhaps a bit altered to compliment his impressive eighty-year-old physique) he wore during that live television appearance.

That evening was what Oprah would call a "Full Circle Moment." I had a deep appreciation for the present moment

I was sharing with my sister, while simultaneously reflecting back on all we had been through.

Often, we don't realize the journey we have been on until a special moment reminds us. It is in times like these that we are often reminded of how far we have come and how lucky we are.

—— ╲ ——

Often, we don't realize the journey we have been on until a special moment reminds us.

That night I was reminded of the luck of the Irish, and how lucky I am to have my Irish Twin, Monica.

CORE-RELATIONS

(Questions to ask yourself)

❧ Is there a relationship in your life, perhaps a sibling or a friend, that you have struggled with, but it has grown stronger over time?

_____

_____

_____

❧ In the space provided, share specifically what had to change in order for that relationship to improve and three ways that relationship has changed for the better.

_____

_____

_____

❧ If you are not in a place to provide the answer to the above question, instead, use the space to write down one relationship you would like to improve and the three ways you will work toward that goal.

_____

_____

_____

COREAGEOUS Challenge: I encourage you to write a handwritten letter to the person who you thought of when asked about which relationship in your life has strengthened over time. It is up to you whether you are ready or not to give that person your letter, but at the very least, write it. I hope you are in a place to send the letter, and if not, it is my hope that one day you will be.

Share your progress on social media to help you stay accountable, using the hashtags: **#COREageous** and **#COREstrong.** If you are more of a private person and prefer not to share online, write down your completion of this **COREAGEOUS Challenge** to help keep yourself on track and accountable.

CHAPTER THIRTEEN

WHAT IT MEANS TO BE COREAGEOUS

The Heart, the OG of Bravery

As a little girl, watching L. Frank Baum's timeless classic, "The Wizard of Oz," I remember feeling so relieved to learn that the Cowardly Lion had his courage, all along. The Cowardly Lion had an authenticity and kindness about him.

As the lion's beautiful story goes on, we learn that he demonstrated acts of courage throughout his entire quest. My relief came in knowing that courage didn't look like any of the grand gestures that society had me believing were necessary. I learned that the true essence of courage extends far beyond what societal expectations place on each one of us (it wasn't just the Cowardly Lion who sought validation by outside means).

The Wizard of Oz was the first memory I had of a story that showed me that courage is not something that can be bestowed upon us by anyone or anything. Rather, it is an intrinsic quality that arises within us when we are our authentic selves and share our hearts with others.

Courage is not something that can be bestowed upon us by anyone or anything. Rather, it is an intrinsic quality that arises within us when we are our authentic selves and share our hearts with others.

Rising to the occasion to be courageous, in big and small ways, and what it means to be **COREAGEOUS** is vast and more meaningful than any shiny medal of valor.

However, grand acts of courage are usually the ones we hear and read about more often, instead of the acts that stick to the original meaning of the word courageous. In one of its earliest forms, the word courage simply meant, "To speak one's mind by telling what is in your heart."

The word courage simply meant, "To speak one's mind by telling what is in your heart."

The acts of courage that I would like to acknowledge here are the everyday choices each one of us makes, to display our hearts. They are the examples of **COREAGEOUS-NESS** that often go unnoticed, so much so, that we may not even realize how brave we, and the peeps around us, really are.

COREAGEOUS CHOICE EXAMPLE № 1
The Hot Flash

Summer, 2023

Now, because this is just the way I roll, I will often use humor to make a point. I really hope you will laugh along with me, and I give you permission to laugh at me when I share this example of what it means to be **COREAGEOUS** and honor what I was feeling, all 1,000 degrees of it!

It was the summer of 2023. It had been one year since my first book was published, and with a dozen or so speaking gigs under my belt, I was beginning to receive offers to speak at various events. Events that included workshops, recovery clinics, small corporate and business settings, athletic groups, and so on.

My son had been a camper at Marty Ogden's Cross Country Running Camp, and our family had also come to know Marty over the last few years of Collin's high school running career. Marty is a long-time cross-country coach who is also featured as a writer on MySportsResults.com as well as Runnerspace.com. The contagious enthusiasm that he brings to the mic when commentating over the high school seasonal championship events has become legendary. The kids love him for many different reasons. For his season predictions, his knowledge, his support, and for the awesomely cool cross-country training camp—The Running Academy—he organizes for them each summer break.

Along with a physical training schedule, games, and lots of memories being made at camp, the runners also have the opportunity to listen to various speakers about topics from college recruiting to training. Some share their own personal experiences as a runner or what they may look for in a runner if they are a coach who is speaking.

When Marty asked me to come and be one of the main speakers at his camp, I was both honored and excited to start planning my presentation.

At the time I was asked to speak, I had nearly finished writing the manuscript for this book and had a solid chapter already written that I could draw from—the chapter about Pivoting. I thought to myself, *Perfect! I'll use that chapter, and just change Life Lesson Number Three to focus more on recovering from an injury, rather than talk about recovering from alcohol addiction.* I wanted to make it relatable for the runners and thought this would be the best path to take.

I had a PowerPoint in place from previous presentations and inspirational storytelling talks I had given that just needed to be tweaked a bit to focus on my message to this group of runners.

On the summer evening of my presentation, we were experiencing a heat wave in New England.

I arrived ninety minutes early to join the campers in the mess hall for dinner, and Marty met me there as well.

"Valerie, slight change in plans," Marty said. "There is a group in the auditorium who are running a bit behind. We can wait or we can do your talk someplace else."

Although the air-conditioned auditorium would have been my first choice, I brushed it off. "No worries, how about I just set up in here," I suggested. Here, meaning the un-air-conditioned mess hall.

I did not mind and being that my whole presentation was about pivoting and adjusting to life's circumstances, I decided that I should practice what I was about to preach and pivot where I would present.

I set up my PowerPoint and got my notes in place. Moments later, the campers began to roll in and claim their seats right in front of me, like I mean *directly* in front of me, which is a key point to note for what took place next.

The first half of the presentation went smoothly, or so I thought, as it is hard to read a room full of teenage boys and girls. They are a tough crowd if you did not know that already. They possess the ability to stare directly into your soul, with zero emotion. Honestly, soldiers who are being interrogated may have reverted to their teenage selves when learning the skills needed for survival during times of torture.

Regardless of the sea of death stares glaring at me, and not knowing if my message was sinking or not, I felt comfortable and smooth, that is until something began to transpire and reminded me that I was a woman of a certain age.

The Hot Flash.

I thought to myself, *Please not now!* As the first beads of sweat to formulate and band together on my forehead, like an army of sweat beads, all banding to soon take over my entire body. *No! For the love of God and all that is holy, please do not go into a full-blown hot flash in front of your son and all of his running friends!*

Too late.

I stand no chance against the army beads of sweat and their massive strength. Thing is, once a hot flash takes hold, sometimes the only way to win is to surrender to what is happening, recognize it, and move on. The all too familiar feeling of warmth that creeps into our bodies, and the army beads of sweat, have no shame in their game. Sometimes you just have to let them win, and then make the decision to move on from the relentless attack of the hot flash.

I was now sweating.

Like I don't mean glistening, perspiration, glow, or sweat under your brow type of sweating. I mean full-on soaked, like I just jumped into a pool kind of sweating. I would have given anything for a cool pool at that moment! But instead, I settled for the cheap brown lunch napkins that Marty kindly began pulling from the dispenser in an effort to save me. Poor guy, trying so hard to help in an increasingly embarrassing and awkward situation.

Had this been happening in a room full of adults, I would have turned it into a joke and used it as a talking point. But these are teenagers, and I am not sure if they even know what a hot flash is. They just see a lady sweating her ass off, inches away from them, trying to get through her presentation.

It was brutal.

I wanted so badly to start over, but there was no way out. There was just one way through, and that was by tapping into my heart center, my **CORE.**

The way through was to be **COREAGEOUS.** To make the choice to take a deep breath, delicately address that I was over-heated, and try my best to get back on course from the hot flash that almost ruined my entire talk.

Embarrassing, to say the least, but I made the choice to keep going and stay focused on the intended message I wanted to drive home to the campers. The kids remained respect-ful. Even with their death stares, no one was laughing or making fun of the situation, and I appreciated their maturity. Embarrassing moments will happen in our lives, and we cannot control them, we can only control our response to them.

> *Embarrassing moments will happen in our lives, and we cannot control them, we can only control our response to them.*

I want to take this moment to shout out to all of my women of a certain age, and all of the **COREAGEOUS** hot flashing moments you have awkwardly been forced to get yourself through. At all the moments you have had to honor the authenticity and audacity of the situation in order to get to the cooler side of things. YOU ARE ALL **COREAGEOUS** MENOPAUSAL WARRIORS TO ME!

COREAGEOUS CHOICE EXAMPLE № 2
The Parent Trap

As most of us who are parents or caregivers know by now, we were not given any handbook, and even if we were, we probably screwed up its directions by now. That is because as a parent, you will inevitably face countless decisions that require you to reach inside and know what is right for your child and your family, despite what outside opinions or handbooks are trying to persuade you to do. You will have to make decisions over and over and avoid falling down the pro-verbial trap of outside expectations. You will make mistakes. You will be disappointed. You will be scared. You will also be surprised. You will be amazed. You will be proud. You will be so in love. You will feel that being a parent or a caregiver to a child is the most sacred blessing any of us could ever have even imagined, and you would do it over again, despite all of the times you faced **COREAGEOUS** choices, with no guarantees that everything will go the way you hope it will for your family.

You will also not find any written materials from this author on how I think someone needs to parent. I will, however, share what it looks like to me, to be **COREAGEOUS** when parenting.

Taking on the responsibility to bring another human into this world, in and of itself, is a very brave thing to do. However, it is the everyday choices, the everyday decisions, and the everyday effort that I have witnessed that have shaped my view of parents as **COREAGEOUS** Warriors.

I think there is not a more **COREAGEOUS** Warrior than the parent(s) or caregiver(s) of a child who is seriously sick or has been diagnosed with a chronic disease. The path this Warrior has to walk is filled with uncertainty, fear, and sleepless nights that add to an emotional state that is already being tested.

These **COREAGEOUS** Warriors become experts in navigating medical terminology, treatments, procedures, and let's not forget, the nightmare of the brutal medical insurance industry. Godspeed to any medical insurance agent or pharmacist, who comes up against a mama who is fighting for pre-authorization for a procedure or lifesaving medication for her child.

There are everyday battles parents and caregivers face that don't include procedures or medicine. They are making brave choices that will put their child's best interests first. Sometimes these decisions are the hardest ones to make, as they tend to be unpopular and may also cause their child to be sad, disappointed, and mad at them for making the tough calls. Calls to keep them home from a birthday party or another fun event if they are having a flare-up in their disease or ailment. Decisions regarding their schooling, travel, social engagements, and commitments, all have to be looked at through a different lens than the lens of a parent with a physically healthy child.

But these are the parents who also become beacons of hope. They are the ones who inspire everyone around them, not because of their constant positivity, but rather, for the quiet strength in their hearts to face another day with grace and resilience. They are the ones who remind us of what it looks like to be selfless, loving, and fiercely devoted to their most precious gifts.

I salute all of the **COREAGEOUS** parents and caregivers who face everyday decisions with the thoughtfulness and bravery it takes to raise the next generation of good peeps. Your choices will help shape the lives of generations to come, so choose wisely but don't worry too much, they're gonna blame us anyways, just ask any therapist!

There are so many **COREAGEOUS** parents who don't fall down the parent trap of decision-making based on outside opinions or societal expectations. Parents who listen to their heart and stay true to what is right for them, and their family.

Like the parent who is about to become an empty nester. Letting go and allowing their children to explore the world independently and make their own mistakes and choices is a hard and **COREAGEOUS** decision as well. It will also look different for every family because we are all individuals, and our needs are not all the same. No, there is no handbook for this one either.

This delicate game of balance is not for the weak of heart. Instinctually, we want to shield our children from pain and suffering, even though we know that we learned most of the valuable and impactful lessons in our own lives through trial and error.

Do our best not to operate from a place of fear, but rather of love.

It's a terrifying stage of life, but also an opportunity to remind ourselves to do our best not to operate from a place of fear, but rather of love. We exert control over what we do not trust, and it is **COREAGEOUS** to make the choice to trust our children and give them freedom to make their own decisions. We are empowering them to carve out their own path for personal growth and development. A path where they will learn how to become their own **COREAGEOUS** selves.

Kudos to all my **COREAGEOUS** empty nesters out there. Hit me up for some Pickleball, for as I write this, my husband and I are less than one year away from this stage as well.

COREAGEOUS CHOICE EXAMPLE № 3
Bravery Does Know Boundaries

One of the things I used to be very guilty of was people-pleasing. Of saying yes to almost anything that was asked of me, especially when it came to volunteering. I now know that was a way for me to feel validated and purposeful. Nothing is wrong with that if you are coming from a solid heart-centered foundation. A foundation where your self-worth isn't based on outside persons, places, or things. It is once we begin searching outside of ourselves, for our own worth, that we are no longer living from our heart center, our **CORE**.

I believe I started living outside of my heart center at a certain point in my life and began overcompensating for something that I was missing. When I got sober, my connection with God and my spiritual faith grew so strong that I no longer looked to anything or anyone to feel love. I began to love myself in a way that was missing before becoming sober of mind, body, and spirit.

With this **CORE-strong** way of living, I began to feel **COREAGEOUS.** I started setting boundaries and became self-aware that this was another important step for me to protect my mental, emotional, and physical health. Constantly saying yes to every request was draining me. When I learned to prioritize where I wanted to spend my time and energy, and pursue things that truly filled my heart, I became able to give back and serve in ways that were more meaningful and impactful.

No longer do I feel that I need to prove myself to anyone. More importantly, no longer do I feel that I need to say yes to every opportunity that comes my way, in order to prove anything to myself.

Rooting self-acceptance and self-worth into how much we are doing, working, achieving, volunteering, cleaning, cooking, doing, doing, always doing, is a dangerous and never-ending hamster wheel of misfortune.

To me, tit is **COREAGEOUS** to know when to say no—to know how and when to establish boundaries—and possess the self-awareness to know your limits in order to protect your **CORE** and not compromise your well-being.

It is COREAGEOUS to know when to say no—to know how and when to establish boundaries—and possess the self-awareness to know your limits in order to protect your CORE and not compromise your well-being.

To me, it is **COREAGEOUS** to stay true to yourself and realize that this is not a selfish thing to do. Rather, staying true to who you are, and having the discernment to know for yourself when it feels right to say yes or to say no to something, is how you live a **COREAGEOUS** life, from your heart.

No, we are not bestowed with courage. Our ability to be **COREAGEOUS** is something that we cultivate over time, mistakes, lessons, and choices. We all have the ability to live a **COREAGEOUS** life. It is a mindset we adopt, a strength that we develop, and a practice we keep practicing, one small step at a time.

You have already taken those small steps throughout this book with each **COREAGEOUS Challenge** you decided to accept. Living a heart-centered, authentic life requires us to make a decision to take action and be disciplined about the things we need to do to live a life that is meaningful to who we are and our purpose. Essentially, before we can give, we must first receive the strength we need to operate from our **CORE**.

In the next and final chapter, I will share the **CORE-strong Tool Kit.**

This tool kit has helped me each and every day to live a life that is **COREAGEOUS,** and you may want to refer to these tools to help you complete your final **COREA-GEOUS Challenge.**

CORE-RELATIONS

❧ Has there been a time in your life when you have been afraid to be your authentic self? If so, when and what were the circumstances?

_____

_____

_____

❧ Was there a time in your life when you felt you had overextended yourself for someone or something that you did not want to say yes to? If so, who or what was it? Why do you think you felt obligated to say yes?

_____

_____

_____

❧ In the space provided, describe what **COREAGEOUS** means to you.

_____

_____

_____

COREAGEOUS Challenge: Here is where you will put it all together. In this final challenge, use the workspace provided to write out your **CORE**. This acronym is to remind you of your personal challenge (goal/crisis), of the outcome you want, of your why, and finally, what tool(s) you are willing to pick up to get what your heart-center (**CORE**) desires.

CORE

> C Challenge (personal goal or crisis)
>
> O Outcome (what is the outcome you want)
>
> R Reason (your why/your purpose)
>
> E Execution (what tools will you pick-up for the outcome you want)

C: _____

_____

_____

_____

_____

_____

_____

_____

_____

_____

_____

_____

_____

_____

_____

_____

O: _____

_____

_____

_____

_____

_____

_____

_____

_____

_____

_____

_____

_____

_____

R: _____

_____

_____

_____

_____

_____

_____

_____

_____

_____

_____

_____

_____

_____

_____

E: _____

_____

_____

_____

_____

_____

_____

_____

_____

_____

_____

_____

_____

_____

Share your progress on social media to help you stay account-able, using the hashtags: **#COREageous, #COREchallenge, and #COREstrong.** If you are more of a private person and prefer not to share online, write down your completion of this **COREAGEOUS Challenge** to help keep yourself on track and accountable.

CHAPTER FOURTEEN

CORE-STRONG TOOL KIT

Progress, Setback, Repeat. Practice, Practice, Practice

THE SPECIFIC TOOLS I reach for, in order to achieve what I am working toward, have varied over time, just as my goals have. For example, remember during lockdown at the height of the pandemic when everyone turned into sourdough bread bakers? There was a mass of baking peeps all reaching for the same tools (Pinterest and YouTube) to discover the sourdough best baking practices. First was demystifying the key to creating a successful sourdough— the starter. We learned that monitoring the temperature and its progress during the days of the dough's sitting period took time and patience. A delicate process, that took a lot of practice as well. But once we figured out what tools we needed to pick up in order to create our well-adjusted baby, our well-loved and absolutely perfect starter, we were ready to bake our bread.

Building and reaching for the life that we want is not that far off from what it takes to make and bake a great sourdough loaf of bread. Both require time, patience, nurturing, and practice. Practice, practice, practice. As we know, nothing great develops quickly. True greatness, or strength of heart (**CORE**) as we have been discussing in this book, is the result of making the decision to take small steps, down a nonlinear path, making gradual progress, while navigating setbacks along the way. I am sure you discovered this for yourself when you took on the various **COREAGEOUS Challenges** at the end of each chapter.

The tools that I reach for are goal-specific and help keep me alive! They are my top go-to tools that I pick up on the daily, to hold on to the strong foundation of who I am, my heart center, my **CORE**. Also, keep in mind, what works for me may or may not work for you. Pick up the ones that do, carry them with you, and pass them along to another because THAT is what life is about, making meaningful connections and sharing our hearts.

CORE-strong Tool Kit:

#1 Connections/Fellowship:

We are social peeps, inherently. Our minds, bodies, and spirits are designed to thrive in a community, and not in isolation. Now I am not saying I don't enjoy alone time; I do. But when I am alone, I am not lonely. Knowing I am not alone, and understanding the importance of making time for connections, nurturing friendships, and having fellowships gives me such peace in my **CORE**, a true blessing from doing the work. Being a part of something bigger than just little ol' me, and maintaining healthy relationships with family, friends, colleagues, and specifically my recovery brothers and sisters, gives me solace. My community of peeps are there to lend support, make me laugh, allow me to cry, and inspire me to do better and be better.

Connections are very important, hence why I placed this tool at the very top. Toward the end of my mother's battle with her depression, I believe it was when she began to isolate herself more that she became sicker and died from her final symptom, by suicide. That is why I feel it is so important as a mental health advocate, to speak and write about the importance of staying connected to peeps. Whether it is just one, or an entire community, we are not meant to be in this world alone, so please remember you are not an island and focus on the work to create the healthy connections you need to be **CORE-strong.**

#2 Spirituality:

This tool is a deeply personal and profound tool, that helps me to connect with God. I can only share what works for me, and what is important for me to do, each and every day, to nurture my spiritual faith. Please know that I respect each person's religious and/or spiritual practices, and I encourage you to find what works for you.

For me, faith is an action word. I try my very best to quite literally do the next right thing to make my father, my God, proud. I try my best to grow and to protect the heart that he gave me. I am not perfect, none of us are, but I live with true intention to practice love and kindness and follow The Golden Rule (treating others the way you would want to be treated). I believe each one of us is on this earth to make connections, to share our hearts and our **CORE**, and that there are many different ways we may honor the purpose God has for each one of us.

I also believe there are many different paths, or maps, that each one of us may use to connect with God. Today, I still feel connected most strongly when I am an "Outsider," trail hiking or road cycling. I continue to put my faith into action through service and volunteering for things that are meaningful to my **CORE**.

At times, these maps still lead me to church and also to temples and synagogues. Other maps include music, hiking, conversations, service, recovery groups, reading, writing, biking, meditation, and prayer.

I still believe there is power in prayer and in meditation, and I continue with the prayer I wrote for myself, (feel free to borrow as you see fit):

"God, please lead me to people, places, and things that continue to bring me closer to you, to my purpose and truth, and ward off anything that doesn't."

I also have my default spiritual practice of meditating on the Serenity Prayer. This practice allows me to "check myself before I wreck myself":

Serenity Prayer

God, grant me the serenity to accept the things
I cannot change,

the courage to change the things I can, and the wisdom to
know the difference.

My spiritual practice is small steps, on the daily, that continue to point me toward **G**ood **O**rderly **D**irection (God).

#3 Movement:

For me, movement is medicine. It is the antidote to keep my anxiety from taking control and brings the fire back into my **CORE**. As a mental health advocate, I am careful not to let my years of personal training and fitness coach language take over and state that we all need to find time to exercise because I have learned that when I use the word exercise, rather than movement, the majority of people I am speaking with, will tune out. I like to remind myself and others that we don't necessarily need intense exercise, (which often is my default) to bring life back into our minds, bodies, and spirits. I am referring to any opportunity we have to move ourselves and avoid remaining stagnant for too long.

When we move, slowly or more fiercely, we release endorphins, or as I like to call them, "endor-funs." These neurotransmitters are produced in our brain and spinal cords and act as a natural pain killer and mood enhancer. When these neurotransmitters release their potent chemical, it packs a punch and floods our brains with feelings of happiness and euphoria.

Movement is literally medicine for our physical and spiritual bodies. Not only acting as a pain killer but also as a mood enhancer. My husband used to encourage me to go out and run, by saying, "You are one run away from a good mood," and usually he was right. Nowadays, I am one hike or bike away from a good mood or way to feel less anxious. Regular movement may help boost our overall mental health and generally boost our temperament, leading to improvements to our total well-being.

#4 Music:

Music has the power to raise our spirits, calm our hearts and minds, and unleash a wide range of emotions, depending on the circumstances we are in. The point is that music is a tool we can pick up to tap into our emotions, allowing us to be our most authentic selves.

Earlier I shared that music has a way of amplifying what is in our hearts, where spoken words may fall short.

It is not just my belief, it is science. Numerous studies have proven that music has a positive state on our mental and physical health. When you are sad, it allows you an opportunity to express that sadness and work through those feelings. When you are happy, a good song will enhance that happiness as well. It is a versatile tool, honoring our emotions or shifting them to a healthier and happier state of mind, if need be.

My playlists are all over the place, depending on the mood I am in, or the mood I am trying to get to. My lists vary from dance party, to inspirational with some rock and roll, old school hip hop, movement motivation, and even a little bit of country. I have also found that I sleep better with music played at a particular frequency, and believe it or not, each frequency even has its own benefits!

The gift of music truly keeps on giving. It is a wonderful tool that I hope you will utilize.

Couple the above tool of movement with music and watch out! There will be no stopping the endorphin party animals inside your **CORE** when these two tools are used together!

#5 Materials:

I am not referring to material things, but rather learning materials. Okay, technically those are things, but I trust you will get the point I am making about having the willingness to keep growing, learning, and remaining coachable.

The materials I have been picking up most recently are Podcasts and Audio Books. Usually on Podcasts, the subject is a deep dive into mental health and preventative measures to stay in good mental health. As far as Audio Books, I love listening to other people's inspirational stories while I am commuting to work. All of our stories matter, and they have the power to heal, motivate, and reassure us that we are not alone in our particular situation.

Learning is not limited to formal education, which honestly never has been for me. I think of it as a lifelong process or discipline that I am blessed to do for myself if I keep my mind open. This growth mindset has allowed me to become more self-aware, confident, and driven; it has given me the ability to set meaningful goals, such as writing books and becoming an inspirational speaker. Having the willingness to remain diligent to pick up materials that will help me to learn and to grow has given me a life that is both fulfilling and authentic to who I am, and who I am becoming. My materials may include books, workshops, YouTube, podcasts, and conversations.

As long as we have the willingness to keep a growth mindset, each of us has the opportunity to discover endless ways to develop a stronger **CORE** and live a heart-centered, **COREAGEOUS** life.

THE END